Handmade Paper Jewelry

Handmade Paper Jewelry

40 Beautiful Projects to Make & Wear

by Heidi Borchers, Candace Liccione & Tiffany Windsor

Sterling Publishing Co., Inc. New York

A Sterling/Chapelle Book

Chapelle, Ltd.:
Jo Packham, Sara Toliver, Cindy Stoeckl

If you have any questions or comments, please contact:
Chapelle, Ltd., Inc., P.O. Box 9252, Ogden, UT 84409
(801) 621-2777 • (801) 621-278
e-mail: chapelle@chapelleltd.com
Web site: www.chapelleltd.com

A Red Lips 4 Courage Book
Red Lips 4 Courage Communicat
8502 E. Chapman Ave., 303
Orange, CA 92869
Web site: www.redlips4courage.com

Library of Congress Cataloging-in-Publication Data available

10 9 8 7 6 5 4 3 2 1
Published by Sterling Publishing Co., Inc. New York
A Sterling/Chapelle Book
387 Park Ave. South, New York, NY 10016
©2006 Heidi Borchers, Candace Liccione, and Tiffany Windsor
Distributed in Canada by Sterling Publishing
c/o Canadian Manda Group, 165 Dufferin St.
Toronto, Ontario, Canada M6K 3H6
Distributed in the United Kingdom by GMC Distribution Services,
Castle Place, 166 High Street, Lewes, East Sussex, England BN7 1XU
Distributed in Australia by Capricorn Link (Australia) Pty. Ltd.
P.O. Box 704, Windsor, NSW 2756, Australia
Printed and Bound in China
All Rights Reserved
Sterling ISBN-13: 978-1-4027-2213-4
        ISBN-10: 1-4027-2213-3

For information about custom editions, special sales, premium and corporate
purchases, please contact Sterling Special Sales Department at 800-805-5489
or specialsales@sterlingpub.com.

Dedication

· · · · · · · · · · · · · · · · · · ·

This book is dedicated
to our mother, Aleene,
who continues to inspire our
creativity. She has taught us,
and a world of women,
how to bring creative
inspiration to everyday life.

Sisters Create

We cannot imagine a day going by without expressing our creativity. As the daughters of craft industry pioneer Aleene Jackson, our lives have been filled with creative opportunities. As we were growing up, we would watch in wonder as Mom's design team transformed supplies into creative craft ideas for women hungry to learn how to re-create projects for their homes, families, and friends.

Many of today's contemporary crafters do not realize that in the early days of the craft industry, no craft stores existed. Through Mom's hard work and determination of never taking no for an answer, small craft sections started popping up in hobby stores across the country.

These mom-and-pop hobby stores started selling the first of what we today recognize as craft items including Aleene's Tacky Glue and flower-making, metal tooling, china painting, and decoupage supplies. To further advance the growth of the craft industry, Mom spearheaded a Craft Caravan in the late 1960s—a truck filled with craft projects and craft instruction books—making stops across the nation.

Growing up in this wonderfully imaginative, intensely creative environment, it wasn't long before each of us girls were teaching classes, running the cash register at Mom's retail store, and developing our own design skills. We're sure that all the time spent in creative work and

Pictured with our mother, crafting pioneer Aleene Jackson, are (from left) Candace Liccione, Heidi Borchers, and Tiffany Windsor.

play gave us the ability to see creativity through different eyes.

As creative studio owners and teachers, we are delighted to join together to celebrate paper. For all the years we have been designing, we've never taken on the challenge of filling a book that transforms everyday papers into jewelry. And what an incredible paper trail this has been.

The focus on paper over these last several years has been a direct result of scrapbooking. New printed papers, textures, colors, layers, and embellishments continue to be introduced, which has inspired the jewelry collections featured throughout this book. But we didn't stop with just scrapbooking papers. Once we started on our paper search, we quickly saw other design opportunities in tissue paper, newspaper, playing cards, and paper flowers.

The first challenge in transforming paper into jewelry is to give it weight. A quick trip to the hardware store provides an immediate remedy for several projects. Also, what might have been a difficult search for the right jewelry findings just a few years ago has turned into a shopping treasure hunt at your local craft store. There are large selections of beads, findings, and jewelry beading kits that complement many of the paper designs featured.

The whole idea behind these projects or any creative project is to make it your own. Personalize with your own colors and style. Regardless of your crafting or beading skill level, you will find jewelry supplies to make your projects fast, fun, and achievable.

We hope you have as much fun making these designs as we had creating them. Enhance your style. Be yourself. Have fun. Get creative. Get inspired!

Heidi   Candace   Tiffany

Table of Contents

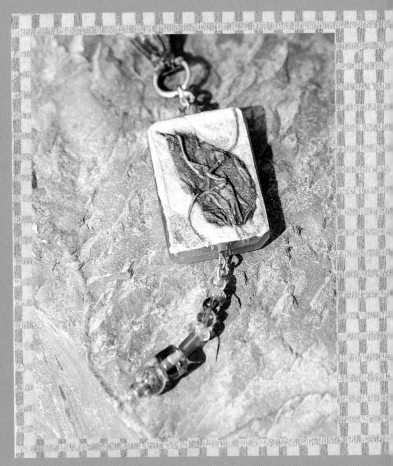

Getting Started

Designing and creating your own jewelry is rich with creative possibilities. Most times when we design, we have a specific outfit in mind to match. Other times, we might find beads or supplies that spark our imagination. With the proliferation of specialty beading stores and bead selections in craft stores, the design possibilities are truly endless.

We have found that many times, our best treasures are discovered when we aren't really looking with a specific project in mind. We'll stumble across the most intriguing beads that we tuck away in our bead jars, knowing that the perfect project will come to life at the right time.

Our jewelry collections are rich with creative crafting techniques—some of which may be new for you. If so, take some time to practice and play with these new techniques, and when you feel comfortable and inspired, you can apply them to creating your project. Remember also that most of the projects featured can be transformed into dozens of other looks just by changing the color scheme. So if you find a project that you like but it is not your color, decide what part of the design captures your fancy and change the pattern to suit your own unique look.

Beading Supplies

BEADS

Metal

Fancy

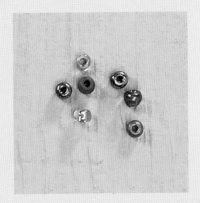

Seed

Faceted

Brass

Crystal

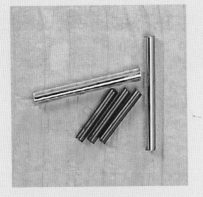

Bugle

Glass

TO STRING YOUR BEADS

Elastic

Embroidery thread

Fancy yarn

Fiber cording

Hemp

Leather

Wire/thread

Jewelry Findings

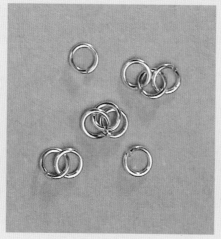

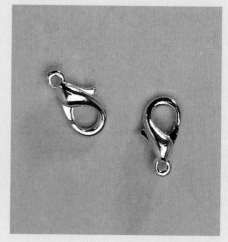

Barrel

Jump rings

Lobster clasps

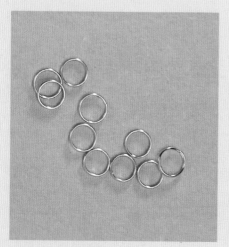

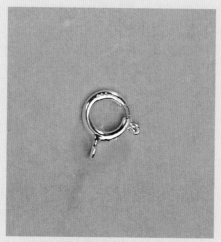

Split rings

Spring clasp

Toggle

Jewelry Findings

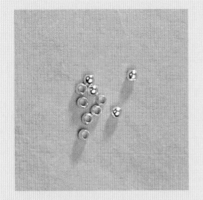

Crimps

Earring hoops

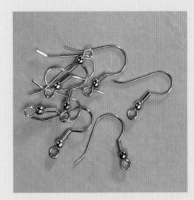

Earring wires

End caps

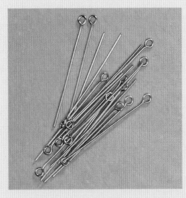

Eye pins

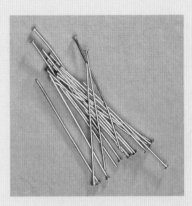

Head pins

Memory wire ends

Spacers

Materials

A quick trip to your local craft store and you will have a basket filled with lots of creative goodies to make your own jewelry treasures.

Acrylic paint: Used to color paper and craft surfaces.

Bamboo skewer: Used to hold paper when rolling paper beads.

Beading wire or thread: For stringing your necklaces and bracelets. Beading wire and thread are available in various thicknesses, depending on the weight of your beads and the size of the holes in the beads.

Beads: Most beads are made from glass, plastic, resin, or semi-precious stones and are available from the smallest Japanese or Czech seed beads up to large resin shapes. (Photo A)

Brads: Metal pieces used to attach two pieces of paper together.

Cording: For stringing necklaces. Leather and suede cording can be found in the leather section of your favorite craft store; elastic cording can be found in the jewelry section.

Cosmetic wedge sponges: Foam sponges used to apply paint or ink.

Craft knife: Sharp cutting tool to cut small or detailed areas.

Craft wire: Available in various colors and dimensions in straight pieces or on rolls. Selection of craft wire will vary by project, depending on use.

Decoupage glue/finish: Specially formulated clear medium designed to adhere paper to a variety of surfaces—a glue and varnish in one.

Embossing heat gun: Used to melt embossing powder.

Embossing ink: Used to hold embossing powder on project surface until melted with embossing heat gun.

Embossing powder: Thick, clear powder melted in dipping pot and used to create look of glass over paper. Also sprinkled over embossing ink and melted with embossing heat gun to create shiny finish.

Embroidery needle: Designed specifically for embroidery with a thicker diameter than a sewing needle. Also known as upholstery needle.

Embroidery thread: For stringing necklaces, embroidery thread can be found in the needle

B

craft section of your favorite craft store. The plys of embroidery thread can be pulled apart depending on the thickness of thread needed for the project. Embroidery thread is available in matte and metallic colors.

Fancy yarns: For stringing and embellishing necklaces. Fancy yarns can be found in the scrapbooking embellishment section of your favorite craft store.

Foamcore: Available at office supply stores in various colors and thicknesses.

Foil: Applied with foiling glue to create shiny metallic finish on various surfaces.

Glitter: Ultra-fine shimmer used to create shiny effect on jewelry embellishments. (Photo B)

Glue: Available at your local craft and hardware stores, many different glues can be used in paper crafting. White craft glue, paper glue, epoxy glue, quick-dry white glue, and hot glue are used to hold together paper and embellishments.

Gold leafing/leaf flakes: Thin sheets of precious metals applied with foiling adhesive glue to provide shiny metallic finish on a variety of surfaces.

Hole punch: Available in a variety of circle sizes and shapes. Used to punch holes in paper for jump rings and eye pins.

Ink: Permanent ink is applied to rubber stamps to create various custom designs and lettering on papers of choice.

Palette: Used to place puddle of glue, paint, or wet medium. Palettes are available in the fine art section of your favorite craft store along with pads of palette paper. Paper or foam plates can also be used as a palette.

Paper: Scrapbook paper, plain and fancy gift wrap paper, handmade paper, watercolor paper, mulberry paper, rice paper, tissue, cardstock, magazine, sheet music, vellum, metallic, foil, and origami are all decorative choices.

Paper gloss: Clear coat used to create glossy final finish over paper surface. Colored paper gloss is used to create a glossy colored finish over paper surface.

Paper lace: Laser-cut paper of various shapes and colors. Traditionally known as paper doilies.

Paper paint: Formulated specifically for paper, paper paint is low moisture and quick drying.

Pipe cleaner: Also known as chenille stem. Used to secure layers of project together.

Pliers: Used to attach, bend, and manipulate jewelry findings. *Left:* Crimping pliers (A); needle-nose pliers (B); round-nose pliers (C).

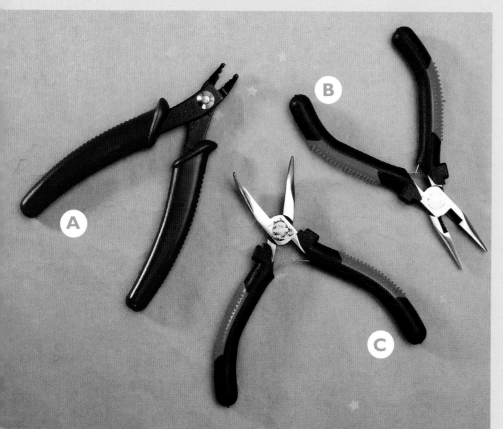

Rubber stamp: Used to apply inked designs to papers.

Sandpaper: Used to rough up slick surfaces so that paint or other mediums adhere to material.

Scissors: Used to cut papers. Decorative edge scissors can be used on paper to create decorative design.

Scoring tool: Used to crease paper for folding. Can also use pen with no ink.

Spray adhesive: Glue in can applied by spraying.

Squeegee: Cardboard mat board used to spread glue or paint on project surface.

Straight pins: Used to pop air bubbles in paper gloss.

Tags: Can be found in office supply stores or scrapbook section of craft stores. Available in fancy papers, cardstock, manilla, or metal rimmed.

Toothpick: Used to hold paper when rolling paper beads.

Varnish: Clear spray-on or brush-on final coat used to provide protective coat on various surfaces.

Washers: Available at your local hardware store in a variety of diameters, washers provide a perfect surface for gluing paper. Washers add needed weight for many paper pendants.

Wire cutters: Used to cut craft wire, eye pins, and flat-head pins.

Tips + Techniques

The key to professional-looking jewelry is to have the right findings and tools. The most important tools you will need when creating jewelry is a pair of needle-nose and round-nose pliers. With a bit of practice, you'll be creating your own bead drops, bead links, and looping eye pins like a professional. Most of the crafting techniques in this book are basic but we've also detailed some techniques that you may not have had the chance to try. Go ahead, have fun—be creative!

Applying foil

Brush foiling glue onto desired area(s). Let glue dry according to package instructions. (This glue remains sticky to the touch even when it is dry.) Press foil into glue and pull up. The foil will stick to the glue.

Applying gloss

When applying gloss to paper, first place paper on waxed paper or other non-stick level surface. Draw a line of gloss directly from bottle around outside edge of design and fill in until entire surface is coated with gloss. Pop any bubbles that appear with pin. Let dry undisturbed overnight. Note that some paper gloss is not compatible with metallic print on papers—metallic ink turns green in some cases. It is best to first test on a sample swatch of paper.

Applying glue

There are several ways to apply glue to your projects. If you are a seasoned crafter, you probably dip your finger into the glue and spread it on your surface. It's quick, easy, and requires just a wet wipe for clean up. You can also use a soft, flat bristle brush or use a squeegee. This method works particularly well on paper. You can cut a squeegee from cardboard mat board or use a credit card. To apply, squeeze glue onto paper. Spread glue into a thin layer with squeegee. For applying glue to small areas, use a toothpick.

Attaching jewelry findings

The key to professionally finished jewelry is to have the right findings and tools. A pair of needle-nose and round-nose pliers are a must and with a little bit of practice, you'll be finishing your own jewelry like the professionals. When using beading wire, attach closure findings with bead crimps. Slide the bead crimp onto the end of the wire then through the eye of the closure and back through the crimp. Pull the end of the wire to tighten the crimp snuggly between the beads and the finding. Use crimping pliers according to package directions to flatten the crimp bead in place. When working with thread and cording you can use a closure specifically designed to crimp around a knot in the thread or tie the cording through the eye of the finding. Add a dab of glue to the knot to secure in place.

Paper Perfected
. . . .
Getting an Aged Look

There are various ways to add an aged look to paper. You can create a tea-dye effect by actually brewing up some strong tea and dipping the paper into the tea. Set paper on absorbent material to dry, using your fingers to smooth out any wrinkles. Excessive wrinkles can be ironed with a hot iron. This tea-dye technique should be done before any stamping. Another quick and easy way to achieve a tea-dye effect is with tea-dye varnish. This is a colored varnish applied after stamping to add a subtle hint of a chestnut color that dries to a shiny finish.

Dry brushing

The key to dry brushing with paint is to remove most of the
paint from your brush. Dip the end of a soft, flat bristle brush
into paint. Brush onto paper towel until most of the paint
is removed. It is always best to start with less paint as you
can always add layers of dry brushing to achieve desired level
of color.

Embossing

Apply embossing ink to designated area. Sprinkle embossing
powder over ink and shake off extra powder. Heat the powder
with embossing gun until powder melts. Let cool. (A)

Making bead drops—flat-head pin

Thread beads onto flat-head pin. Snug pin against the last bead
on the pin, then fold over end at 90-degree angle with flat-head
pliers. Cut excess to approximately $1/4$". Using round-nose
pliers, grasp end, curling around pliers to create eye.

Making bead links—eye pin

Thread beads onto eye
pin. Snug against the last
bead on pin, then fold
over end at 90-degree
angle with flat-head
pliers. Cut excess to
approximately $1/4$". Using
round-nose pliers, grasp
end, curling around
pliers to create eye.

Making loops on eye or flat-head pin

Thread beads onto pin. Snug against the last bead on pin, then fold over end at 90-degree angle with flat-head pliers. Cut excess to approximately $1/4$". Using round-nose pliers, grasp end, curling around pliers to create eye.

Test before you create

You might want to first create one test piece to be certain that your craft wire does not change color. Some wires are affected by glue and/or gloss. To test, glue wire to plain white paper, then set aside to dry. Apply gloss over wire and set aside to dry. If wire maintains its original color, it's OK to proceed. If the wire changes color, you may want to consider incorporating this unique look into your project.

Using paper clay

Remove paper clay from package and tear off a piece of clay. Place remaining clay in zip-top bag as paper clay can dry out quickly. Knead clay to smooth consistency and mold into desired shape and size. You also can roll paper clay on smooth non-stick surface and cut with cookie or clay cutters. To smooth edges, dip your finger in water and run along edges of paper clay shape. Return leftover clay to zip-top bag. Let paper clay dry overnight. You can file any rough edges with an emery board or fine sandpaper.

Paper Perfected

Paper Gloss & Metallic Inks

Paper gloss can provide a pretty finishing touch and protective surface over fine papers. When working with metallic papers, you should always test for compatibility with your paper gloss as some gloss and/or varnishes can turn the metallic ink a different color. (Usually a very pretty patina green.) Apply your paper gloss to the paper and let it dry completely to determine if it is compatible with the metallic ink.

Bracelet   Locket

Lapel Pin

Necklace   Earrings

Paper Jewelry Projects

· · · · · · · · · · · · · · · · ·

From handmade mulberry to origami, we've taken pieces of
fanciful paper and transformed them into beautiful jewelry
projects. So whether your style is Zen, Nature-Inspired,
Feminine, or simply Just for the Girls, we invite you to get
creative and get inspired!

Zen Inspiration

CHAPTER ONE

Cool, calm, reflective, peaceful, quiet. These are all ideas of how Zen affects our lives. For many years, we have immersed ourselves in spiritual studies, which we always tap into whenever we need to find our space of Zen—whether it's to quiet the mind after a busy day or to find a creative center.

Simplicity is the most prominent characteristic of Zen, but we smile when we think of our creative simplicity. Most of the time it simply doesn't exist for us. Our creative space is usually a mass of clutter—we can't seem to stick to just one project at a time. We go into this creative space where nothing else exists, where there are no other distractions. It's a total focus on creativity. It's a space where one idea starts, and then the next and the next and the next. So, naturally, our creative work space reflects those creative ideas that just keep flowing.

We simply start grabbing supplies and the next thing you know, we're lost in creative inspiration. This is creative Zen for us. The results are some really great projects and a really messy dining room table. The strange thing is that in every other part of our lives, we love order and organization. But not when it comes to crafting.

Inspired by calming style and color, we have worked to capture the essence and qualities that speak the simplicity of Zen in this paper jewelry collection. So, turn on some soothing music, breathe in the calming fragrances of aromatherapy, and let your creative Zen come to life.

Metal Washer

NECKLACE

Above: A washer covered with paper, cording, and beads are the basic materials for this pendant.

Right: The leather cord necklace is slipped through a short strand of diminutive beads tied around the pendant.

Materials

> 2" metal washer
> Bead string
> Beads: decorative glass or semi-precious stone
> Cording: leather
> Craft glue

> Paper: scrapbook paper with gold printed design
> Paper gloss: clear
> Pencil
> Scissors or craft knife

Instructions

Cut paper to 2 ⅜" circle. Apply glue to one side of washer. Place paper over glue, and gently press paper into glue. Snip along edges every ⅛" and fold excess paper to back of washer.

Glue paper edges to back of washer, carefully pressing paper to lay flat on washer. Snip inside circle in same manner and fold excess to back of washer.

To finish back of washer, using washer as pattern, trace shape onto wrong side of paper. Cut slightly smaller than tracing line around outside and inside pattern lines. Apply glue to back of washer and glue paper onto washer, gently pressing out any bubbles. Set aside to dry.

Apply paper gloss to front of decorated washer. Let dry overnight. Turn over and repeat application on back of washer. Let dry overnight.

String beads to create 3" loop. Thread through center of washer and tie bead strand to washer. Attach necklace findings to leather cording and string through bead loop.

Paper Perfected
. . . .
Using Everyday Hardware

Metal washers can be found in a variety of shapes and sizes at your local hardware store. They provide a unique and inexpensive base to this necklace. The weight of the washer also allows the jewelry to hang nicely from your chain of choice. If your style is feminine, opt for a floral paper that is sturdy enough to cover the washer. Paper gloss provides the perfect finishing touch for this museum-quality piece.

Left: An everyday washer serves as the base for this tranquil pendant, giving it both shape and weight.

Simple household items can become attractive jewelry when covered with decorative paper. A humble washer is just the right size to make a pendant, and its weight helps make it hang perfectly from a cord or chain.

Serenity Disks

Materials

- > Cording: gold
- > Craft glue
- > Jewelry findings: earring backings, necklace closure
- > Large embroidery needle
- > Metal tags: various sizes
- > Metallic thread: gold
- > Paper: origami, mulberry
- > Pencil
- > Scissors

Instructions

Using each metal tag as a guide, trace patterns onto back of paper. Cut ¼" larger than pattern line. Apply glue to back of paper and place on metal tag. Snip paper every ⅛" along edge and wrap excess to back of tag, applying more glue if necessary. Let dry.

Above: Small metal tags in several sizes can be found with scrapbooking supplies.

Right: While these earrings are clip-on, it would be just as easy to adhere earring posts for pierced ears.

Use needle to poke hole through hole in tag. Stack tags and thread together with metallic thread. Tie into knot and cut off excess. Add dab of glue to knot to secure. Let dry. String on cording. Attach necklace closure.

To make earrings, repeat process with desired washers. Glue backings to backs of earrings. Let dry.

Paper Perfected
· · · · · · · · · · ·

Getting a Smooth Finish

To create a clean, rounded edge
along your metal tag, snip paper
every ⅛" and wrap around
to the back of the tag. This
will allow you to overlap the
snipped edges in order to
keep the paper lying smooth.
This project is great for
recycling small paper scraps.

*Left: Each layer of the Serenity
Disks Necklace is covered with
coordinating origami paper.
While blue was our color of
choice, the jewelry set would be
just as stunning in red or green.*

The multitude of tags and embellishments made for the
scrapbooking market can also be used for paper jewelry.
Metal tags in several sizes are sturdy enough
to cover with paper and will not warp.

Layered Circles

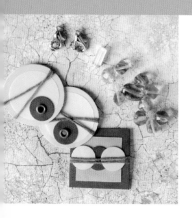

Above: Embellished paper tags and colored beads make bracelet charms.

Right: Embellishments hang from this bracelet by lobster claws.

Materials

> Beads: small green

> Craft glue

> Extra-small hole punch

> Jewelry findings: jump rings, lobster claws

> No. 140 watercolor paper

> Paper paint and brush (optional)

> Pre-decorated circular scrapbook tags

> Scissors

> Silver link bracelet

> Spray varnish (optional)

Instructions

Glue tags onto watercolor paper. Let set 10 minutes, and then cut out along tag design line. Press edges of papers together to assure secure bond. Set aside to dry. If desired, paint watercolor paper (back side of circles) to complement color of tags.

Any embellishments that are too lightweight can be glued to cardstock or watercolor paper for added stability.

Punch hole for jump ring. Attach lobster claw to jump ring. Unlatch tags from bracelet and hang on necklace chain for interchangeable design.

Optional: To protect your paper charms, you may need to spray on a light coat of clear varnish. Or for a shiny finish, add a coat of paper gloss.

Scrapbooking Embellishments

A shopping trip to your local craft or scrapbook store will uncover a treasure trove of paper designs that can be easily transformed into last-minute jewelry ideas. Many of today's scrapbooking embellishments are already layered, glued, styled, and ready to go. Also, many embellishments can be glued back-to-back. This design concept lends itself well to bracelet charms that will be seen from both front and back.

Left: This silver bracelet provides just enough space between links to hang alternating bead drops and colorful circular tags.

Paper accents and glass beads complement each other. They are a great combination also because the weight of the beads compensates for how light the paper is. Colors can match or contrast, depending on the look you want to create.

Mirror Tile

Above: Small round glass mirrors are covered with origami paper to create this bracelet.

Right: Only the sides of the circular mirrors are covered with paper.

Materials

> Beading crimp pliers

> Beading wire

> Beads: glass

> Craft mirrors: small, round

> Jewelry findings: bracelet closure, crimp beads

> Paper: origami

> Pencil

> Quick-dry glue

> Scissors

Instructions

Use mirror as pattern to trace and cut origami papers. With quick-dry glue, adhere to one side of mirror. Set aside to dry.

To assemble bracelet, attach bracelet closure to one end of beading wire with crimping bead. Slide on several glass beads. Place glue on undecorated side of two mirrors.

Place beading wire down center and glue two mirrors together. Be sure to abut them against glass beads.

Continue to add glass beads and glue mirrors together until desired length is achieved. Attach closure to end of bracelet with crimp bead.

Paper Perfected
. . . .
Adhering Mirror Pieces Together

Quick-dry glue or five-minute epoxy glue can be used to quickly hold the mirror pieces together, which are glued directly onto the beading wire. You may wish to lay out your mirror pieces and beads before you string them together to ensure uniform spacing between each element.

Left: A rich and exotic look is easily created with exquisite and intricately detailed origami paper.

Small mirror crafting tiles are weighty and are a good shape to work with. You may wish to etch the glass of the mirrors for a completely different look.

33

Painted Gloss Charms

Above: Painted paper, jump rings, and glass beads are basic components of this simple necklace.

Right: Aqua beads are strung onto lavender paper cording. Knots are made between each bead to keep the paper charms and beads in place.

Materials

> Beads: medium aqua, small aqua
> Cardboard squeegee
> Clear paint jewels
> Ink: lavender pigment
> Jewelry findings: crimp beads, eyelets, jump rings, necklace closure

> No. 140 watercolor paper
> Paint gloss: clear, lilac quartz, turquoise, white pearl
> Paper cording: lavender
> Ruler
> Scissors

Instructions

Squeeze paint gloss onto watercolor paper. Spread gloss colors over entire paper using cardboard squeegee. Let dry overnight.

Repeat on reverse side. Let dry overnight. Cut into 1" squares or desired shapes. Attach eyelets, and then attach jump rings.

Cut paper cording to desired length. String beads to create pattern of one medium aqua bead, one small aqua bead, and one paper charm, making small knot between each item to keep them in place. Add necklace closure to ends.

Paper Perfected
Designing With Colored Gloss

When creating these paint gloss pieces, start with watercolor paper at least 8 ½" x 11", which will give you plenty of space to swirl and marble the gloss colors. Play with the gloss for different effects—from smooth, soft colors to thick swirls. You can also drip additional gloss onto the paper for a more textured look.

Left: Watercolor paper serves as the base for the paper charms, which are painted and attached to the necklace chain with eyelets and jump rings.

You don't need to be a watercolor artist to match favorite paint colors to create jewelry that coordinates with your wardrobe. If you are looking for just the right hue for a special outfit, practice mixing custom paint colors.

Flower Medallion

NECKLACE

Above: Metallic-finish paper gives the medallion dimension.

Right: Glass beads are slipped inside fine mesh tubing, which has been knotted to create a unique necklace.

Materials

> Beads: medium glass oval
> Craft glue
> Craft wire
> Decorative edge scissors
> Dimensional scrapbook medallion embellishment
> Epoxy glue
> Jewelry findings: jump ring, necklace closure

> Metallic ribbon tubing
> Paper: decorative scrap paper, heavy textured metallic hand-made cardstock paper
> Scissors
> Small hole punch
> Ultra-fine crystal glitter

Instructions

Cut 2" disk from metallic cardstock with decorative scissors. Glue paper embellishment over disk. Coat with epoxy and sprinkle with crystal glitter.

Cut 1" length of craft wire. Fold in half and twist ends to create loop. Glue loop on top back of disk. Cut strip of paper and glue over twisted end of wire to help hold in place.

Slide beads into metallic ribbon tubing. Knot between each bead. Hole punch top of medallion and add jump ring.

Add disk to center of necklace and continue to add beads into ribbon tube. Attach necklace closure to ends.

Made to Order

With the cutting, layering, and decorations already complete, it's easy to transform scrapbook medallions into jewelry medallions. Just shop the scrapbook aisle at your favorite craft store to find page embellishments that are suitable for jewelry. Select embellishments that are created on cardstock or heavier papers for the best durability.

Left: Ready-made scrapbook page embellishments are used to create this fashionable pendant.

Fast-drying craft epoxy can be used to cover most types of paper. Be generous with the amount you use to create a sturdy and attractive pendant. Adding seed beads gives the piece a colorful detail that refracts light.

Mosaic Picture Frame

Materials

> Beads: glass round, faceted, and tube
> Decoupage glue/finish
> Jewelry finding: necklace toggle closure
> Mini frame pendant with cord
> Paper: fancy gift wrap or scrapbook
> Scissors
> Soft, flat bristle brush

Instructions

Cut or tear papers into small pieces. Brush glue onto outside of frame and press papers into glue. Brush glue over papers. Repeat to cover entire outside surface. Let dry.

Repeat to cover inside frame area of mini frame. Let dry. Find center of cording and cut. Add beads and necklace closure. Be sure to tie small knots between beads to keep them in place.

Top: Small kraft paper frames are available at craft stores.

Above: The toggle clasp is a decorative choice for a necklace clasp.

Left: Open this pretty pendant to reveal framed photos.

Left: Torn paper scraps and decoupage transform kraft paper frames into a wearable trinket.

Paper crafters know to keep all sorts of scraps of paper, no matter how small. It doesn't take much of any one paper to piece together a colorful paper mosaic cover for a frame or locket.

Paper Box

Above: A simple paper box is transformed with beautiful paper and gold thread.

Materials

> ½" soft bristle brush
> Asian-themed lucky coin
> Beads: small glass
> Craft glue
> Embossing heat gun
> Embossing ink pen
> Embossing powder: gold

> Embroidery needle
> Embroidery thread: gold
> Gold leafing adhesive
> Jewelry finding:
   necklace closure
> Mini papier-mâché box

> Paper: fancy gift wrap,
   origami, or scrapbook
> Scissors
> Toothpicks
> Variegated gold and copper
   leaf flakes

Instructions

Open box to separate pieces. Brush gold leafing adhesive on outside of box lid and outside of box bottom. Cover adhesive with leaf flakes according to label instructions. Set aside to dry. Repeat to cover inside of box.

Measure and cut paper to fit inside bottom of box. Glue in place. Measure and cut paper to fit lid of box, cutting slightly smaller than box. Glue in place.

Apply embossing ink around outside of paper and scattered around paper print design. Sprinkle with embossing powder, then melt powder with embossing gun. Repeat around inside edge of box bottom. Glue coin in box. Carefully poke hole into top of box, just below lid, to create hole for threads.

To create paper bead, cut paper to 3" x ⅜". Cut to point at one end to create long, tapered triangle piece. Place print side down on flat work surface. Place toothpick at flat edge and roll paper over toothpick to create bead. Apply glue to end of paper to hold in place. Slide paper bead off toothpick. Repeat to create desired number of beads. Set aside to dry.

Slide all beads onto thread, knotting to keep them in place. Slide ends of cording through hole in box and tie in knot to secure. Add necklace closure to other ends of cording. Place lid back on box.

Left: While we tucked an Asian-themed coin in our Paper Box Locket, you may wish to store a small sentiment or encouraging words in your Zen-inspired box.

A small box can be used as a locket to hold a memorable treasure or sweet surprise. A coin or good luck charm can be glued inside to add weight to the box.

Look-of-Glass Beaded

Materials

> Craft glue

> Craft wire

> Heat gun

> Jewelry finding:
  necklace closure

> Metallic foil

> Paper: gift wrap

> Toothpick or wood skewer

> Ultra-thick embossing powder
  and melting pot

Instructions

Cut paper into small strips at slight angle, using pattern shown below. Apply dab of glue to large end of paper strip. Place toothpick over end and roll paper strip to create bead. Glue pointed end of paper to secure in place. Remove toothpick. Let glue dry.

Heat ultra-thick embossing powder according to package directions. Slide toothpick onto end of bead. Roll and dip bead into ultra-thick embossing powder.

Note: Ultra-thick embossing powder will probably "string" at this step but this is OK. Let bead sit for 3-4 minutes.

Cut ⅛"-thick strips of metallic paper. Place dab of glue on each end and roll metallic paper around bead. Roll and dip bead into ultra-thick embossing powder. Let bead sit for 3-4 minutes.

Heat bead surface with heat gun until it starts to melt. Continue to turn bead until entire surface is clear and relatively blemish free. String beads to create necklace. Add necklace closure.

Top: Embossing powder and metallic paper create one-of-a-kind beads.

Above: Paper strips encapsulated in embossing powder allow you to create your own beads.

42

After dipping your paper bead into ultra-thick embossing powder, leave it on the end of the skewer for a few moments and then carefully use another skewer to slide it off and then onto a non-stick surface. Set aside to cool. Be careful when handling the bead as it will hold the heat for quite some time. Remember that irregular shapes and textures make beads look handmade.

Left: When dipped in embossing powder and heated with an embossing gun, these beads take on the beauty and imperfections found in handmade glass beads.

When you create handmade beads with paper and embossing powder the final result will look like the work of a glass artisan. The more exotic and unique the papers you use, the more distinctive the beads will be.

Textured Paper

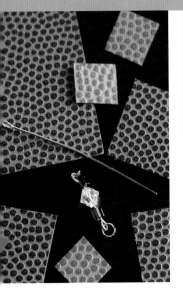

Above: Textured papers we chose have the look of leather.

Right: Each square disk can be accented with a rhinestone, crystal, or glass bead.

Materials

> Beads: glass, rhinestones, or Swarovski crystals

> Craft glue

> Hole punch

> Jewelry findings: eye pins, small jump rings, gold-finish necklace chain

> Needle-nose pliers

> Paper gloss

> Pin: corsage or straight sewing

> Scissors

> Scrapbook paper: basketball texture, football texture

Instructions

For each section of necklace, cut two 1" squares from paper. Cut one ⅝" square of contrasting color for center. Punch hole in center of ⅝" square.

Apply glue to wrong side of one 1" square. Place eye pin diagonally from corner to corner. Place second 1" square over glued paper, pressing firmly along edges to hold together. Trim edges if needed.

Glue ⅝" square in center. Glue bead in center. Repeat to create seven squares.

Squeeze paper gloss over surface. Let dry overnight. Turn squares over and coat with gloss. Let dry overnight. Trim eye pin and turn end with pliers to form loop. Repeat with each square.

Attach squares and beads to small jump rings, and then gold-finish necklace.

Combining Papers

Textured papers provide a unique design element. These papers were originally made to replicate basketball and football skins. This combination of papers, however, takes on a more exotic look. When you're scouting out different papers—whether they are scrapbook or gift wrap papers, or even photocopied pages from a book—consider the many bejeweled items that may be crafted.

Left: Eye pins, dotted with beads, link the square disks to each other to form the Textured Paper Necklace. Paper gloss gives the disks a clean, finished appearance.

With the wide variety of papers available, you will find some embossed to look like leather, suede, and wood. Also look for papers with heavy embossing in floral and nature motifs.

Zen Gift Wrap

Top: Small gift wrap scraps make great jewelry.

Above: While these earrings are circular, you may want to replicate the square form of the pendant.

Materials

> ¾" metal washers: 3

> 1 ½" washer

> 2" washer

> Assorted beads (optional)

> Beading wire

> Craft glue

> Craft knife

> Jewelry findings: earring posts, jump ring, necklace chain, necklace closures

> Metallic print gift wrap

> No. 140 watercolor paper

> Paper gloss: clear

> Scissors

Square Pendant Necklace
Instructions

Cut watercolor paper into 1" square. Apply glue to watercolor paper. Place ¾" washer in glue. Apply glue to top of washer. Center gift wrap over washer and press into glue, squeezing papers together with fingers to conform to shape of washer. Glue gift wrap to back of watercolor paper. Set aside to dry. Puddle paper gloss in middle of washer shape and drop bead into gloss. Set aside to dry. Attach eyelet in corner. Attach jump ring to hang as pendant, and then attach necklace closure to ends.

To make earrings: Repeat process for necklace using ¾" washers to create two matching earrings. Attach earring posts to back of disks.

Round Pendant Necklace
Instructions

Glue 1 ½" and 2" washers together. Set aside to dry. Cut gift wrap to 2 ¼" circle. Spread glue over top of washers and glue paper in place, pressing paper to take on shape of top washer. Snip edge of paper every ⅛", wrap around edge, and glue to back. Cut slits in center with craft knife. Wrap cut paper to back side of pendant and glue in place. Set aside to dry.

Coat top and outside edge of pendant with paper gloss. Drop beads along edge of smaller washer into wet gloss. Cut circle of gift wrap and glue to back of pendant to cover washer. Loop necklace chain through pendant. Attach necklace closure.

Left: The Square Pendant Necklace (right) and earrings and the Round Pendant Necklace were made with washers available at your local hardware store.

Next time you open a beautifully wrapped gift and are tempted to toss the wrapping paper, think again. It only takes a few small pieces to make a paper necklace and earrings. What better way to remember the presentation of a wonderful gift?

Nature Inspiration

As young girls growing up in Southern California, we spent our long summer days discovering the outdoor sanctuary known as our backyard. Our mother is passionate about gardening and she loved unwinding from her hectic work schedule by spending time tending to her plants and gardens, and she shared that passion.

To us, some of the garden work seemed, well, like work. Pulling weeds, mowing lawns, and raking leaves were sometimes a bit tedious for three free-spirited youngsters. We would have rather been climbing trees, peeking into bird nests, digging up earthworms, or playing Red Light, Green Light on the front lawn.

As we reflect on all our outdoor memories, we are so grateful for these experiences that have made such an impact on our life endeavors. Our favorite times are spent outdoors in nature. As a medicinal herbalist, Candace relates nature to healing. For many years, she tended to seven acres of herbs, sharing her plant passion through healing workshops and counseling.

Nature can be expressed in many ways to complement our fashion styles. We had such fun reflecting on our lifetime of nature memories and finding papers and creative styles that ignite thoughts of nature—from the soft prints of flora and the whimsy of fauna, to the bright, solid greens of springtime and the warm colors and textures of autumn.

Amber-Hued

Above: Colored resin tiles can be found in bead stores.

Right: Earring posts are safe and secured with jewelry glue.

Materials

> Beads: resin, medium square ceramic, spacer

> Craft wire

> Decoupage glue/finish

> Handmade fiber paper: amber, ivory, fern green, orange

> Jewelry findings: crimp beads, earring posts, necklace closure

> Jewelry glue

> Sandpaper: fine

> Scissors

> Soft, flat bristle brush

Instructions

Cut fiber paper in small pieces. Gently sand surface of resin beads. Apply decoupage glue to surface and lay papers on top, overlapping in random pattern. Cut off excess paper to fit bead. Brush coat of decoupage glue over top of papers. Set aside to dry.

Cut craft wire to desired length of necklace. String small glass spacers, medium ceramic, and large resin beads in desired pattern. Attach crimp beads and necklace closure to ends.

Create beads for earrings in same manner. Glue earring posts to back of bead with jewelry glue.

Paper Perfected
. . . .

Layering Colors & Textures

The key to gluing papers on ready-made resin beads is to lightly sand the surface to create "tooth" for the glue to hold on to. The beauty of this project is the layering of paper colors and textures. For custom colored papers, slightly thin paper paint with water to create a wash of color over neutral rice paper or mulberry paper. You can brush, dip, or spray the thinned paint onto your paper. Let the paint dry completely and then tear papers into small pieces.

Left: Small spacer beads and ceramic beads let the larger embellished resin beads be the focal point on the Amber-Hued Necklace.

Using handmade papers gives jewelry projects a texture that cannot be attained with commercially made papers. Mulberry paper works well because it can be pulled apart to create ragged edges.

Golden Leaves

Top: Resin tile beads come in many colors.

Above: While we chose earring posts, clip-on backings also could be used.

Materials

> Acrylic paint: gold metallic
> Beading wire
> Beads: resin, small glass round
> Decoupage glue/finish
> Handmade textured paper: green, ivory, leaf designs

> Jewelry findings: crimp beads, earring posts, necklace closure
> Jewelry glue
> Sandpaper: fine
> Soft, flat bristle brush
> Thread: gold metallic

Instructions

To create bead, gently sand surface of resin bead. Cut paper to shape of bead. Apply decoupage glue to surface and layer papers.

For leaf, cut or tear to desired shape. Lay in decoupage glue and slightly wrinkle for textured effect.

Brush on coat of decoupage over top of papers. Press in metallic threads randomly. Set aside to dry. Lightly dry brush gold metallic paint over surface. Set aside to dry.

Cut beading wire to desired length of necklace. String small glass spacers and large resin beads in desired pattern. Attach crimp beads and necklace closure to ends.

Create beads for earrings in same manner. Glue earring posts to backs of beads with jewelry glue.

Paper Perfected

Getting a Textured Look

For more textural designs, you can select heavier or textured papers. For the look of veining in leaves, tear your leaf design, aligning the texture in the paper to create the impression of veining. You also can manipulate papers once they have "soaked" in the decoupage medium. After you have torn your design into the shape and size you desire, dip your shape into decoupage and place it on the sanded resin bead. Use your fingers or the end of a toothpick to move the paper to create slight folds and peaks.

Left: Handmade textured paper brushed with metallic gold paint gives the Golden Leaves Necklace its foliage theme.

Soft shades of green textured papers take on a golden hue when lightly dry brushed with gold metallic paint. For a different look, rub on copper or silver metallic paste for beautiful burnished effects.

53

Beaded Drop

Materials

> Acrylic paint: gold metallic
> Beads: resin, small and medium glass
> Decoupage glue/finish
> Jewelry findings: eye pin, flat-head pin, necklace closure
> Needle-nose pliers
> Paper: leaf design
> Ribbon
> Sandpaper: fine
> Scissors
> Soft, flat bristle bush

Instructions

To create leaf bead, gently sand surface of resin bead. Cut paper to shape of bead. Apply decoupage glue to surface and lay in paper.

Above: Hand-dyed ribbon and tapes make an interesting hanger for a pendant made with a resin bead, glass beads, and jewelry findings.

Right: Extend the length of your necklace by adding a multi-hued bead drop.

To shape into pendant, thread resin bead onto eye pin. Form loop at end. To create beaded drop, stack assorted glass beads onto flat-head pin. Attach beaded drop at bottom. Attach loop to necklace closure loop.

Thread ribbon with needle-nose pliers. Tie large round bead to one end of ribbon. Tie loop in other end, slightly larger than large round bead. Slip round bead through loop to create necklace.

Simplicity is the key to this design, where you can include your own collectibles to provide the finishing details. Fancy ribbons and yarns, whether new or vintage, are great choices. If you want to wear this pendant on a shorter length, simply slide the ribbon off and tie on another. You can also make the beaded drop interchangeable with a small lobster claw attachment to change out the beaded drop to match a particular outfit or season.

Left: Decoupage medium acts as both a glue and a varnish to adhere paper to the surface of the resin bead.

This small pendant is such a joy to make. We looked to nature for inspiration and came up with a resin bead decoupaged with a leaf design. Since the beauty is in the details, we chose a vintage silk ribbon for the necklace and a warm selection of colors for the beaded drop.

Stamped Paper Tags

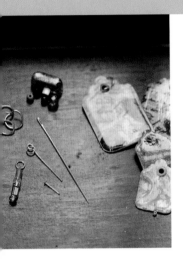

Above: Tags adhered with decorative paper, beads, and jewelry findings are the base of these paper tags necklaces.

Right: Antique sheet music provides an interesting backing to this tag.

Materials

> Beads: small glass, assorted colors
> Cording: waxed linen or satin, or beads strung on beading thread
> Cosmetic wedge sponge
> Craft glue
> Heat gun
> Ink: permanent pigment
> Jewelry findings: eyelets, jump rings
> Paper gloss: clear
> Rubber stamps: various designs
> Scissors
> Sheet music
> Tags: various sizes

Instructions

Apply ink to rubber stamp images and stamp on one side of tag in desired designs. Heat set ink with heat gun.

Apply ink to cosmetic wedge sponge and dab ink along edges of tags for aged look. Glue sheet music cut to fit back side of tag.

Attach eyelet to tag. Apply paper gloss to one side of tag. Let dry overnight.

Apply paper gloss to reverse side of tags. Let dry overnight. Attach tags to cording with jump rings. Tie cording at ends in knot.

Paper Perfected
· · · · · · · · · · ·
Overcoating Images

When stamping, in most instances we are seeking clean, crisp, stamped images. But for an added design element in achieving a vintage effect, experiment with overcoating your stamped images with paper gloss before the ink is dry or the heat is set. This can result in a slight bleeding look, which can be very effective. Also, if the ink is not completely dry, the paper gloss can crackle, which may also create a very pretty effect.

Left: It's easy to create one-of-a-kind pendants from manilla shipping tags. Create your chain with plain cording or string beads for a more dazzling look.

Decorating small tags with rubber stamps, favorite images, and a soft color wash is easy and doesn't take much time. Each tag becomes a work of art, and serves as the centerpiece of a lovely necklace.

Gold Paper Lace

Materials

> Cosmetic wedge sponge

> Embossing or heat gun

> Gold paper lace: various designs

> Jewelry findings: pin backs

> Paper gloss: clear

> Permanent stamping ink

Instructions

Apply ink to paper lace with wedge sponge, dabbing and spreading to achieve desired color coverage. Use heat gun to heat set ink.

To strengthen paper, apply paper gloss to back of paper lace design by squeezing from bottle directly onto back. Press pin back into gloss while still wet. Let dry overnight.

Above: Foil cutouts are made in many motifs.

Right: A quick application of permanent inks transforms gold paper lace into beautiful hues of shimmering metallic.

Paper Perfected
· · · · · · · · · · ·
Using Paper Doilies

Paper doilies have changed over the years into some very intriguing design opportunities. These delicate treasures take on a whole variety of jewelry looks, depending on how they are colored. You will want to experiment with different permanent inks as each brand takes on its own unique coloring and opacity. Another interesting effect is to apply clear embossing ink and colored embossing powders, which meld together in the heating process for a beautiful metal look.

Left: In bright jewel tones or subtle pastel inks, these paper lace lapel pins reflect the essence of iridescence.

We happened upon these dainty lace doilies and decided they would make interesting lapel pins. All that was needed were some distinct color patterns and paper gloss to strengthen the paper lace.

Butterfly-in-Flight

Above: Gift wrap is a great source of interesting images. Small beads add texture and interest.

Materials

> Beads: seed and no-hole micro beads
> Butterfly printed gift wrap
> Craft glue

> Craft wire (3" length for each butterfly)
> Jewelry findings: eye pins, jewelry chain
> Needle-nose pliers

> No. 140 watercolor paper or heavy cardstock
> Paper gloss: clear
> Scissors
> Toothpick

Instructions

Fold wire in half with pliers to create antennae. Add seed beads and curl ends to hold beads in place. Cut two matching butterfly shapes from gift wrap. *Note:* At this step, you do not need to cut out exact design.

Glue first design to watercolor paper. This will be front of design. Leave area where antennae will be attached.

While glue is wet, cut along butterfly pattern edge. Press cut edges together until glue holds edges securely. Measure and cut eye pins to fit down center of body.

Apply glue to back of watercolor paper and place eye pins in center. Lay second butterfly pattern over glue and press all three layers together to work out any air bubbles.

Carefully cut away excess paper from design. Apply glue to fold of antennae wire and slip between butterfly paper and watercolor paper. Press cut edges together until glue holds edges securely.

Determine design for micro beads. Apply glue with toothpick to those design areas. Sprinkle glue with micro beads, shaking off excess beads. Set aside to dry.

Apply paper gloss to front surface. Let dry overnight. Apply paper gloss to back of butterfly paper. Let dry overnight. Attach to chain.

Left: Gift wrap paper provides the decorative design for these butterflies while micro beads add the decorative detail.

Lovely printed images are everywhere, including on gift wrap paper. If there is a motif you enjoy, such as a butterfly, bumble bee, or ladybug, it's easy to make a necklace to share the object of your affection.

Look-of-Copper

Above: Use patterns supplied or make your own.

Right: Glue on a pin back and transform these Look-of-Copper shapes.

Materials

> Brown grocery bag
> Craft glue
> Craft wire: copper
> Foil and foiling glue
> Jewelry findings: pin backs

> Pencil
> Round-nose pliers
> Scissors
> Transfer paper

Instructions

Leaf Pin

Trace leaf pattern (see page 65) onto brown bag. Glue two layers of bag together. While glue is still wet, cut out pattern.

Press cut edges together after cutting. Apply line of glue down center of leaf. While glue is still wet, give dimensional shape to leaf by gently molding with your fingers. Set aside to dry.

Following package instructions, apply foil adhesive. Let dry until tacky. Apply foil. Glue on pin back.

Paper Perfected
· · · · · · · · · · · · · · ·
Getting into Shape

Today's contemporary metallic foils lend themselves beautifully to custom jewelry pins. Some foils come in full multicolored sheets while others are actual flakes. A brown bag is an excellent paper to use to create any shape. Craft glue provides just the right amount of moisture to soften the paper in order to mold it into various shapes while still maintaining its strength.

Left: Add dimension to the paper pin by pressing with your finger while the glued layers are still wet. These pins are ideal companions for lapels, hats, and scarves.

Paper can be transformed to look like many other materials. Foiling kits are available in a range of metals and can be easily applied to paper as basic as a paper grocery bag.

63

Top: Children's coloring books are a great resource for simple patterns such as this dragonfly.

Above: Multicolored foil adhesives provide an interesting color pattern on the Sunburst Pin.

Dragonfly Pin

Trace dragonfly center body pattern (see page 65) onto brown bag. Glue two layers of bag together. While glue is still wet, cut out pattern.

Trace wings pattern (see page 65) onto brown bag. Glue two layers of bag together. While glue is still wet, cut out center body pattern. Press cut edges together.

While glue is still wet, give dimensional shape to center body piece and wings by gently molding with your fingers.

Glue center body shape in place. Set aside to dry. For dimensional line, apply line of glue around wings and across center body. Set aside to dry.

Following package instructions, apply foil adhesive. Let dry until tacky. Apply foil. Bend craft wire in half and curl ends to create antennae. Glue in place. Glue on pin back.

Sunburst Pin

Trace sunburst pattern (see page 65) onto brown bag. Glue two layers of bag together. While glue is still wet, cut out pattern.

Trace center sun pattern onto brown bag. Glue two layers of bag together. While glue is still wet, cut out center sun circle pattern. Press cut edges together.

While glue is still wet, give dimensional shape to center sun circle pattern and sun rays by gently molding with your fingers. Glue center circle shape in place. Set aside to dry.

For dimensional line, apply line of glue around circle and through center of sunrays. Set aside to dry.

Following package instructions, apply foil adhesive. Let dry until tacky. Apply foil. Glue on pin back.

Patterns

We have supplied an extra pattern in the shape of a lizard, but any little critter would make an interesting lapel pin. You only need to look to Mother Nature to find all sorts of inspiration.

Look-of-Ceramic Fish

Top: Foam board and fancy yarns are the key ingredients to this necklace.

Above: The tip of a cotton swab is an easy way to add stripes.

Materials

> Acrylic paint: Coastline Blue, Dark Foliage Green, Green Tea, Lavender, Phthalo Blue, Rainforest Green
> Beads: small glass, assorted colors
> Cotton swabs
> Craft glue
> Craft knife
> Fancy yarns and fibers
> Fine-tip bristle brush
> Foam board
> Jewelry findings: eye pins, jump rings, necklace closure
> Needle-nose pliers
> Pencil
> Scissors
> Soft, flat bristle brush
> Spray gloss varnish

Instructions

Trace fish onto foam board. Cut along pattern line with craft knife. Apply several coats of glue to entire front, back, and sides of fish, letting glue dry in between coats. This will give softer edge to cut edges of foam board.

Using photo as guide, paint fish assorted colors. Set aside to dry. Spray varnish over painted surface. Set aside to dry.

Cut eye pins to ½" in length. Dip cut end into glue. Use pliers to poke eye pins into mouth end of fish. Set aside to dry.

To make necklace: Select 6-8 strands of yarn and cut to desired length, keeping in mind that when yarns are braided, length will shorten. Loosely braid strands together to create necklace. If thicker necklace is desired, add more lengths of yarn.

Knot ends to secure while completing necklace. Attach bead drops with jump rings to strands at random sections of yarn. Select necklace closure specifically designed to grasp and close around all strands. Attach fish to necklace with jump rings.

Paper Perfected
· · · · · · · · · ·
Using Foam Board

Foam board makes a great beginning surface for a variety of jewelry shapes. The challenge is always in how the edges look after you have cut them— especially in detailed shapes. The key to transforming that cut-edge look is to apply many coats of glue to soften and seal the edges.

Left: Fancy yarns and fibers are braided and looped to create a lush, tropical "chain" for the catch of the day.

Using foam board, colorful craft paint, and a photo or print as inspiration you can create charms in any shape. Colorful fish mixed with beads in tropical colors make a cheerful summer necklace.

Playing Card

Materials

> Beads: small glass

> Cording

> Craft glue

> Embossing heat gun

> Embossing ink and powder

> Jewelry findings: pin backs, jump rings

> Paper gloss: clear

> Scissors

> Scrapbook tags: metal or cardboard

> Vintage playing cards

Above: Vintage playing cards can be found in a variety of flora and fauna designs.

Right: Apply embossing ink and powder along the edges of the metal tag for a pretty transformation from silver to gold.

Instructions

Cut card motifs to fit inside scrapbook tags. Glue in place. Set aside to dry. Apply paper gloss. Let dry overnight. Repeat if desired.

Apply embossing ink to metal rim. Sprinkle with embossing powder. Heat with embossing gun. Set aside to cool.

For lapel pins, adhere pin backs; for pendants, attach jump rings then thread cording through hole at top. Finish with glass beads secured in place with knots at each end.

Vintage Appeal

Over the years, we have used vintage playing cards in many collage and paperwork projects. The designs are intriguing and, when teamed with metal scrapbook tags, create instant vintage pins. For an even more aged effect, after gluing the cards into the tag frames, apply a two-step crackle finish that will make these pieces look like they have been tucked away for decades.

Above Left: Teamed with red beads and black cording, this floral design takes on a vintage look.
Left: Smaller elements are perfect for lapel pins.

Vintage playing cards often have wonderful images that can be transformed into beautiful paper pendants or lapel pins. Souvenir playing cards from a favorite destination can be fun to use too.

Plain Decoupage Bracelet

Materials

> Cosmetic wedge sponge
> Decoupage glue/finish
> Paper paint

> Soft, flat bristle brush
> Tissue paper: white
> Wood bracelet

Instructions

Apply paper paint to tissue in random patterns with bristle brush and/or cosmetic wedge sponge. Set aside to dry.

Tear tissue into strips and small pieces. Brush decoupage onto wood bracelet. Press tissue into decoupage and brush decoupage over tissue to hold in place. Repeat to cover entire bracelet. Place on raised non-stick surface. Set aside to dry completely.

Decoupage Necklace + Earrings

Materials

> Beading wire
> Beads: small glass, metal leaves
> Cosmetic wedge sponge
> Decoupage glue/finish

> Foil and foiling glue: metallic multicolored
> Jewelry findings: crimp beads, earring hooks, eye pins, necklace closure

> Paper paint
> Soft, flat bristle brush
> Tissue paper: white
> Wood bead necklace
> Wood skewer

Instructions

Dismantle wood bead necklace. Apply paper paint to tissue in random pattern. Smooth with cosmetic wedge sponge. Set aside to dry completely.

(Continued on page 72)

Top: Decoupage medium adheres bits of paper to wood beads.

Above: When strung with leaf embellishments, these wood beads take on the look of fall fruit.

Left: Handmade paper scraps
torn in random patterns can be
decoupaged onto a variety of
wood shapes for your fabulous
fall wardrobe.

Just about any surface can be covered with paper,
including wood beads. Choosing beautiful
papers to achieve a decoupage treatment will
create lovely necklaces, bracelets, and earrings.

Above: Tiny beads and metallic foil are glued onto this once-plain wood bracelet to create an interesting pattern.

(Continued from page 70)

Tear tissue into small pieces. Brush decoupage onto wood beads of necklace. Press tissue into decoupage and brush decoupage over tissue to hold in place. Repeat to cover entire bead.

Place bead on wood skewer to dry. Apply foiling glue in light random pattern on bead. Let set according to package directions. Apply foil.

String wood and small glass beads and metal leaves on beading wire to create necklace by adding closure with crimp beads or eye pins to create earrings. Embellish earrings with small glass and leaf beads. Attach earring hooks.

Decorated Decoupage Bracelet

Materials

> ¼"-wide double-stick tape
> Beads: no-hole micro
> Cosmetic wedge sponges
> Decoupage glue/finish

> Foil and foiling glue: metallic multicolored
> Handmade grid paper, foiled
> Handmade mulberry paper

> Paper paint
> Scissors
> Small bowl
> Soft, flat bristle brush
> Wood bracelet

Instructions

Apply paper paint to handmade paper in random pattern with brush and/or cosmetic wedge sponges. Set aside to dry.

Tear paper into strips and small pieces. Brush decoupage onto wood bracelet. Press paper into decoupage and brush decoupage over tissue to hold in place. Repeat to cover entire bracelet. Place on raised non-stick surface. Set aside to dry completely.

Cut strip of grid paper to desired size, then decoupage onto surface. Cut foiled paper into strips. Glue in place. Set aside to dry.

Apply double-stick tape in desired pattern. Pour beads into small shallow bowl. Press tape into beads. Shake off excess beads.

Following package instructions, apply foil adhesive around grid paper. Let dry until tacky. Apply foil.

Paper Perfected

· · · · · · · · · ·

One-Step Decoupage Finishes

A fine decoupage finish originally required great time, skill, and patience while multiple layers of decoupage were applied, dried, and then carefully sanded. Today's one-step decoupage finishes allow for quicker, more artistic interpretations of the original decoupage process. One-step decoupage finishes can be applied like glue to adhere papers and then coated over the top as a sealer. Tissue papers and mulberry papers work well with the decoupage technique.

Left: Add some interest to a plain bracelet with a row or two of multi-colored micro beads.

Outdated plastic bangle bracelets can step back into style with a decoupage paper finish. Choose hues that coordinate with your wardrobe.

Fall Leaves

Above: Die-cut leaves and metallic leaf flakes make projects easy.

Right: Look for the smallest metallic paper leaf for a lapel pin to match the Fall Leaves Necklace.

Materials

> Beads: glass drops, rounds, tubes

> Cardstock: heavy handmade

> Craft glue

> Craft wire

> Die-cut paper leaves

> Embroidery thread: metallic copper

> Epoxy glue

> Jewelry findings: necklace closure, pin back

> Paper: metallic solid

> Scissors

> Variegated metallic leaf flakes

Instructions

Glue paper leaves to cardstock. Using paper leaves as pattern guide, cut out. Apply thick coat of epoxy. While glue is still sticky, drop metallic leaves into glue in random pattern. Set aside to dry. Apply second coat of epoxy. Set aside to dry.

To create hanger for leaves, cut 1" length of craft wire. Fold in half and twist ends to create loop. Cut small strip of paper. Glue to back of leaf over twisted wire. Set aside to dry.

Cut thread to desired necklace length. Thread through loop on back of focal leaf. Tie thread into knot approximately 1" up from top of leaf. Add bead and knot.

Split threads and continue to add beads and leaves until desired length is achieved. Attach necklace closure.

To make lapel pin: Glue on pin back.

To add realistic dimension to leaves, while epoxy is drying, gently bend paper leaves to shape them. As the epoxy can tend to be sticky while drying, you can use craft tweezers or toothpicks to help guide the shaping. You also can tuck a pencil under each side of the leaf to hold the shape while the epoxy is drying.

Left: Paper of all different textures and weights are decorated with metallic leaf flakes for these fabulous fall charms.

The flaming beauty of changing leaves is replicated by adding metallic flecks to die-cut paper leaves in subtle brown and copper colors.

Fabulously Feminine

CHAPTER THREE

Growing up, we loved our dress-up playtimes, and we still enjoy dressing up today. A fond memory we treasure is the time spent playing in our grandmother's jewelry boxes. We loved the colors, textures, and beauty of the costume jewelry that filled those boxes as we held those treasure pieces in our hands.

Tiffany loved to organize, so her time was spent lining up all the pretty pieces in their proper places. We would all giggle as Candace tried to play "grown-up" as she embellished herself with as many pieces of jewelry as her tiny hands, ears, and neck would hold.

We smile in sweet reflection as we now see how those early childhood playtimes would reflect on how jewelry would play into our grown-up worlds. Heidi still loves the beauty, colors, and design of jewelry.

So how does the look of fabulously feminine work in today's fashion world? Feminine dressing can take on a variety of looks, from romantic florals in soft, light, and breezy designs, to sassy, bold, flirty, and playful mix-and-match statements that express personal style. The elegant sophistication and enchantment of glamour reflects days gone by and fashion icons such as Audrey Hepburn and Marilyn Monroe, encapsulating breathtaking beauty and luxury.

Inspired by our family's costume jewelry treasures and incorporating today's style, we have captured the essence of these family stories in this fabulously feminine paper jewelry collection.

Silk Ribbon

Above: Silk paper ribbon and vintage beads are used to create these fanciful pins.

Right: While we chose beads and crystals, you may embellish the center of your paper flower with a small piece of antique jewelry.

Materials

> Craft glue

> Gold cording

> Jewelry findings: pin backs

> Needle and thread

> Paper ribbon

> Scissors

> Vintage beads
  (for flower pin)

Instructions

Bow Lapel Pin

Fold paper ribbon to create bow. Wrap with cording to secure in center, tying cording ends in back to secure in place. Glue or tie pin back in place on back. Fluff ribbon loops and cut streamer ends to desired length.

Flower Lapel Pin

Fold end of paper ribbon back approximately 1 ½" to create first loop. Repeat to create matching loop. This is first layer of flower. Repeat looping ribbon back and forth, increasing size of loop with each layer until desired finished size of flower is completed.

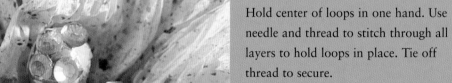

Hold center of loops in one hand. Use needle and thread to stitch through all layers to hold loops in place. Tie off thread to secure.

Gently re-arrange any loops that may have shifted. Glue beads and crystals to center of flower. Glue pin back on back of ribbon flower.

*Left: Paper ribbon takes on
a softer side when looped into
a pretty posy or bow. To finish off
the flower, vintage beads have been
sewn in for stamens.*

Paper ribbon made to replicate the soft feel of silk is available
in the gift wrap section of many craft stores. The soft texture
of the paper together with its ability to hold a shape makes it
a perfect candidate for paper flower or bow lapel pins.

Memory Box

Materials

> Beads: glass faceted and tube
> Craft glue
> Decorative brad
> Embroidery needle: large
> Gold cording
> Jewelry finding: necklace closure
> Matchbox

> Paper: decorative embossed, metallic abstract sticker paper
> Paper towel
> Rub-on gold leaf paste
> Scissors
> Thread: gold metallic
> Vintage photo

Instructions

Create bead drop on looped thread for bottom of box. Create beaded cording length for top of box. (This should be measured and cut to create desired length of necklace.) Set aside.

Separate matchbox pieces. Measure and cut paper strips of metallic sticker paper and attach to edges of outside box. Measure, cut, and glue embossed paper to top and bottom of outside of box.

Apply gold paste by squeezing small amount on fingertip. Wipe excess onto paper towel and gently wipe remaining paste over embossed paper.

Measure, cut, and apply metallic paper to fit around outside of inside box. Cut corners to create clean mitered edge. Use needle to carefully poke hole through top and bottom.

Attach bead drop to bottom of box by pressing brad through hole and catching end of bead loop. Open brad ends to secure in place. Cover brad ends on inside of box with strip of matching paper glued in place. Repeat process for top of box.

Cut and glue vintage photo in place inside box. Set aside to dry. Slide box pieces back together. Attach necklace closure to ends of necklace.

Top: Blank matchboxes can be purchased at craft stores.

Above: Photograph treasures and trinkets can be hidden in this magical matchbox.

Left: Heavy embossed textured papers come to life when antiqued with gold leaf paste. Poke a hole at the bottom of the box and string a few fancy beads.

A matchstick box with a slide-off cover makes a delightful pendant. Cover the box with your paper of choice and glue a favorite family photo inside. The paper can be brushed softly with gold leaf paste for an elegant effect.

Notary Seal

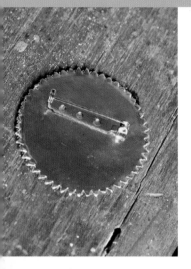

Above: To convert your notary seal, simply glue on pin back.

Right: Any type of vintage seals or stickers make fun paper jewelry.

Materials

> Craft glue

> Epoxy glue

> Jewelry finding: pin back

> Metal disk

> Metallic pen: gold

> Vintage notary seals:
 gold and red

> Vintage-style floral stickers

Instructions

Glue gold notary seals over each side of metal disk. Glue red notary seal over each gold seal, offsetting spikes so that both red and gold can be seen along edge.

Place sticker in center of seal. Use metallic gold pen to highlight areas of sticker. Coat with epoxy glue. Set aside to dry. Glue on pin back.

Optional: For other color choices, cut circles from paper that has been painted with paper paint. Rather than flower stickers, you may prefer a mosaic design, fauna, or some other favorite image clipped from a magazine or old book.

Creating an Official Seal

The paper used over the gold notary seals is actually the spacer paper found in the box of notary seals. It gives the effect of natural brown paper. The same effect could be achieved with other lightweight natural papers.

Or create your own look of notary seals from metallic papers. These papers can be found in a variety of colors and can be cut along the edges with decorative edge scissors.

Left: Floral cutouts provide a focal point for these vintage-inspired pins. An epoxy coating adds the perfect luster for an enameled effect.

Vintage notary seals have wonderful pointed edges and can be embellished with just about any cutout image. Old gummed star seals are another option for making a lapel pin.

Grandmother

LAPEL PIN

Materials

> Embossing heat gun

> Embossing ink

> Embossing powder: gold

> Epoxy glue, varnish,
  or paper gloss

> Jewelry finding: pin back

> Laser-cut paper blanks

> Papers: handmade metallic print

> Vintage photo (or copy)

Instructions

Apply embossing ink to laser-cut paper. Sprinkle with embossing powder. Use embossing tool to melt powder. Repeat procedure to emboss entire back side of laser cutout.

Glue several layers of varying sizes of decorative paper to front center. Glue photograph to paper. Let dry completely.

Apply epoxy, varnish, or paper gloss over photograph and decorative papers and set on non-stick surface to dry. *Note:* Do not apply epoxy over laser-cut areas. Glue on pin back.

Top Left: Laser cutouts on cardstock work best. Middle Left: If you prefer a more sturdy lapel pin, adhere a heavier weight paper to the back before embossing. Left: Delicate lace papers can be transformed into the look of intricate metal when coated with embossing powders.

A favorite photograph of a special family member can be showcased on a lapel pin that is sure to encourage happy memories. Laser-cut paper templates look like intricately hand-worked metal when covered with heavy embossing powder.

Say a Little Prayer

LAPEL PIN

Materials

> Craft glue

> Embossing heat gun

> Embossing ink pen

> Embossing powder: gold

> Embroidery thread: metallic

> Jewelry finding: pin back

> Mini buttons

> Mini envelope

> Paper: decorative, scrapbook, or gift wrap

> Pencil

> Scissors

> Scoring tool

> Sewing needle

Instructions

Write small message on decorative paper. Open mini envelope and use as template to draw envelope pattern on decorative paper, aligning bottom flap with printed message. Cut out along pattern lines. Score folds.

Apply embossing ink along flap edges. Sprinkle with embossing powder. Use embossing gun to melt powder.

Stitch buttons to envelope with needle and one strand of metallic thread. Cut small length of two strands of metallic thread and wrap around buttons for closure. Use dab of glue to hold ends of thread together. Tuck special note inside envelope. Glue on pin back.

Top Right: Miniature note paper and envelope are the basis of the pin. Middle Right: The note is opened to reveal a favorite biblical passage. Right: Sweet words of support are always at hand when tucked inside this envelope.

A small envelope that holds a secret message or a small blessing makes a thoughtful gift for a friend. Use a small envelope for a template and cut your own from pretty paper.

Forget-Me-Not
NECKLACE

Above: A small blank book hung from embroidery thread can be purchased at a craft store.

Right: The miniature pages may be inscribed with special sentiments or quotes.

Materials

> Bead: green glass
> Computer, scanner, and printer
> Craft glue
> Decorative brad
> Embroidery needle

> Embroidery ribbon: pale yellow
> Embroidery thread: black metallic
> Jewelry finding: necklace S-hook closure

> Mini-book necklace
> Paper: metallic sticker sheeting
> Scissors
> Vintage postcard

Instructions

Scan vintage postcard into computer. Reduce image to mini-book size, then print. Measure and cut to fit book cover.

Cut two 1" pieces of embroidery ribbon. Fold to create loop. Dab with glue to hold. Cover outside of mini-book with metallic sticker sheeting, tucking both ribbon loops in place under sheeting. (One loop goes on backside and one at back top.) Glue print on front of book.

Poke hole through book cover where brad will be placed. Press brad through hole and open to secure. Glue decorative paper over brad ends to hold in place. Close book and loop ribbon over brad.

Loop embroidery thread through top ribbon loop. Tie knot in thread approximately ⅜" from loop. Thread both strands of thread through bead. Tie knot above bead. Split strands and tie to necklace closure.

Paper Perfected

. . . .

Vintage Postcard Sources

Vintage postcards are a great resource for images along with old family photos or turn-of-the-last-century advertisements. With a quick check on-line, you will find a wealth of resources to purchase beautiful collections or individual vintage cards in all types of themes. Also be sure to check through your family archives, where you might find some fabulous treasures.

Left: A vintage postcard serves as the book cover of the Forget-Me-Not Necklace. A pretty glass bead coordinates with the colors in the postcard.

A small notebook decorated with a portion of a vintage postcard makes an attractive and practical pendant. Scan the image and print it out on matte paper, then cut it out and adhere to the front of a small book.

Cast Paper

Top: Glass beads are best because they give the project weight.

Above: The earring backs are secured with craft glue.

Materials

> Beading crimp pliers

> Beading wire: copper

> Beads: glass and metallic spacer

> Casting paper

> Craft glue

> Embossing heat gun

> Embossing ink

> Embossing powder: gold

> Jewelry findings: crimp beads, earring backs, necklace chain with closure, bracelet closure

> Needle-nose pliers

> Paper: metallic

> Paper mold: pendant size, bracelet size

> Round-nose pliers

> Scissors

> Spray paint: copper

Instructions

Prepare cast paper according to package directions. Press paper into mold. Let dry according to package directions.

Cover paper shapes with spray paint. Let dry. Apply embossing ink randomly to design. Sprinkle with embossing powder. Melt powder with embossing gun.

For bottom of pendant, create bead drop for bottom from wire loop. String on beads. Secure end with crimp bead.

For top of pendant, create bead drop from wire loop, large enough to thread chain through. Secure beads in place with crimp bead. Slide pendant on necklace.

For bracelet, string beading wire through closure and secure with crimp bead. Add spacer beads and glass beads to wire. Lay beading wire centered over paper shape. Cut metallic paper to size of paper shape. Glue in place over beading wire, securing paper shape to wire. Be certain paper shape is snug against beads.

Repeat process with spacer beads, glass beads, and paper shapes for desired length. Secure remaining end of closure onto beading wire with crimp bead. For earrings, glue on earring backs.

While many craft stores sell cast paper molds, we used a clay push mold for this jewelry set. Clay molds are easier to find and are available in a wider variety of designs. A hair dryer can be used to dry the paper, however, excessive heat may warp the mold.

Left: Decorative molds provide the distinct detailing in this hand-cast paper jewelry set. Gold embossing powder brings out the detail of the pendant.

Paper can be easily shredded in a blender and then cast into countless shapes. There are molds available just for paper cast making, but you can also use clay molds. Use a hair dryer to speed the drying process.

Vellum Tag

BRACELET & EARRINGS

Above: Vellum tags can be stamped or painted.

Right: Tags are transformed into earrings with earring hooks.

Materials

- > Cosmetic wedge sponges
- > Heat gun
- > Hole punch: small
- > Jewelry findings: earring hooks, jump rings
- > Metal bracelet

- > Needle-nose pliers
- > Pigment ink: cranberry, light pink
- > Rubber stamp: floral and words
- > Vellum paper tags
- > Wet wipes

Instructions

Apply light pink ink to back of paper vellum tag. Dab with cosmetic wedge sponge to soften color. Set ink with heat gun.

Apply cranberry ink to stamp, press front of vellum tag into inked stamp. Remove excess ink from metal tag edge with wet wipe. Set ink with heat gun. Punch hole in top center, then attach jump ring. Attach to bracelet.

Create earring tags in same manner. Punch hole in vellum and attach jump rings and earring hooks with pliers.

Paper Perfected
. . . .
Working with Rubber Stamps

The key to working with rubber stamp images is to get them placed exactly where you want them on your design. The easiest way to achieve this is to ink the rubber stamp design and set the stamp, face-up, on a level working surface. Pick up your vellum tag and press it onto the stamp exactly where you want to pick up the inked design. Carefully lift the tag to reveal the stamped image. For crisp images, re-ink your stamp before stamping each image.

Left: Lightweight and colorful, the Vellum Tag Bracelet and Earrings are created with decorative stamps and vellum scrapbook tags.

The translucent nature of vellum allows light to pass through the paper, making it a great paper to work with when fashioning beautiful jewelry. Vellum tags can be purchased in many sizes and shapes.

Paper Mosaic

Above: No paper scrap is wasted in mosaic art.

Right: The cardboard shape is transformed into a lapel pin simply by adding a pin back.

Materials

> Acrylic paint: black, color of choice (for "grout")
> Bamboo skewer
> Cardboard shapes: small
> Craft glue
> Jewelry findings: pin backs

> Paper: gift wrap or scrapbook, metallic foil
> Paper gloss: clear
> Paper paint
> Scissors
> Soft, flat bristle brush
> Toothpick

Instructions

Paint front of cardboard shape desired color. Set aside to dry. Paint sides and back. Set aside to dry completely.

Cut papers into desired shapes to create designs. For heart-shaped pin, cut heart from paper, then cut heart into mosaic-shaped pieces. Using toothpick, apply glue to backs of paper.

Add single layer of black dots around edge with black paint and bamboo skewer. Place onto cardboard shape, pressing out any air bubbles and excess glue. Let glue dry.

Apply paper gloss. Let dry overnight. Adhere pin backs with glue.

Optional: Embellish center of floral design with bead or rhinestone.

Left: From tiny snips of paper, you can craft intricate miniature mosaic designs in hues that suit your fancy.

Paper Perfected
. . . .
Picking up Small Shapes

A tip for picking up small pieces of cut paper and aligning them in your finished design is to dip the tip of a toothpick in a small amount of glue. Dab off excess glue so that just a small amount is sticky on the end. Then, press the toothpick onto the small piece of paper to pick up item.

Small bits of beautiful paper can be pieced together onto the shape of your choice when making a pretty pin. If the pin is a gift, work with the recipient's favorite colors or a particular holiday theme.

Foam Board Hearts

NECKLACE

Above: Gift wrap paper gives jewelry its charm.

Right: Choose a variety of glass bead shapes and sizes to give weight to this necklace.

Materials

> Beads: assorted glass, bugle, and faceted

> Craft glue

> Craft knife

> Craft wire (optional)

> Foam board

> Jewelry findings: eye pins, jump rings, necklace closure

> Needle-nose pliers

> Paper: gift wrap or scrapbook

> Pencil

> Scissors

> Straight pin

Instructions

Draw 8-10 heart designs on foam board. Cut along pattern line with craft knife. For fronts of heart, cut paper ½" larger than heart design.

For backs of heart, cut paper ⅛" smaller than heart design. Apply glue to back of front piece of paper. Place onto foam board heart. Snip every ⅛" and fold excess over sides and back. Glue back paper to back of heart.

Poke hole through paper at top of heart with straight pin. Cut eye pin to ½". Dip cut end of eye pin into glue and press into top of heart. Attach jump ring to eye pin. Repeat with each heart.

For added embellishment, thread beads onto craft wire. Wrap wire around hearts using pliers to swirl ends.

To create necklace: Cut 4 strands of craft wire desired length. String assorted beads and hearts in desired pattern. Attach necklace closure.

Getting Wired

Craft wire adds a pretty layer of detail to many designs. A bit of practice yields beautiful results. First, cut a 24" length of craft wire. Swirl end of wire with pliers. Thread 12 beads onto the wire, holding the swirled end of wire in place. Start wrapping wire around design, moving beads into place along length of wire. Keep wrapping until finished effect is achieved. Cut remaining wire and swirl cut end.

Left: Gift wrap paper adds a decorative finishing detail to foam core, creating the designer look of ceramic hearts.

Hearts make a warm, romantic design for a vintage-inspired necklace. Foam board can be cut easily with a sharp craft knife and covered with decorative paper, or if you prefer you can paint or draw on the cutouts.

95

Ceramic Tile

Above: Resin craft tiles are sold in bead departments of craft stores and bead stores.

Right: Mix and match papers for this quick and easy cut-and-glue project.

Materials

> Beading crimp pliers

> Beading wire

> Beads: small faceted glass, tiles

> Craft glue

> Jewelry findings: crimp beads, toggle clasp

> Paper: fancy metallic

> Paper gloss: clear

> Pencil

> Scissors

> Soft, flat bristle brush

Instructions

Measure, cut, and glue paper onto tiles. Let glue dry completely overnight. Apply paper gloss over papers using bristle brush. Let dry completely overnight. If desired, repeat application of paper gloss for extra-thick effect.

String tiles on beading wire with glass beads in between. Anchor to toggle clasp with crimp beads and pliers.

Optional: For added variety to your tile bracelet, decorate both sides of the tiles for a reversible bracelet. Keep in mind that the bead color will show on each side so you will need to select papers that have at least one color in common for this reverse tile project to work.

Getting it Right

This is a quick and easy project but you must be patient while each of the steps dries. If you apply the paper gloss too soon over wet paper, it can have a tendency to crack as it dries. When selecting beads for this project, keep in mind that many different sizes and shapes can be used, but the faceted beads fit closer to the straight edge of the tiles.

Left: Interesting gift wrap or origami papers provide the look of hand painting on these look-of-ceramic bracelet tiles.

Craft tiles can be purchased with a set of holes drilled through them, which makes it a cinch to string together. The tiles become instant beauties when covered with attractive handmade papers.

For the Girls

CHAPTER FOUR

Whether it's expressing our wild and funky side with today's edgy retro looks or a pulled-together sophisticated style, from 13 to 93 there is still a bit of girl in each of us.

A look back over the decades brings about many incarnations of today's fun looks for teen jewelry. From natural neutrals to hippie prints—subtle shimmer to after-5 sparkle, it's all about incorporating your own personal expression into your wardrobe.

How do you make your own signature style memorable? For some of us, it's in the colors we choose for our accessories. Bright primaries perk us up, jewel tones soothe us, and neutrals say, "Look at me," in a quiet way. Regardless of how you look at it, when we express ourselves through jewelry accessories, it's about creating a memorable statement.

For all you girls out there, we say, "You go girls." Experiment, have fun, get girly—get creative. A quick trip to the craft store will bring lots of creative ideas for girls of all ages to create unique jewelry accessories. Coated wires and paper alphabet letters are transformed into personalized monograms, scrapbook charms become a groovy girlfriend gift, glitter goes glamorous, and tiny flowers speak retro charm.

Glitter Flower

Above: Flower-shaped tags come in various sizes. Glitter in different colors is available at craft stores.

Right: A smattering of ultra-fine glitter dresses up these paper flower cutouts, which are layered to form this Glitter Flower Lapel Pin.

Materials

> Acrylic paint: mauve
> Beads: crystal or rhinestone, green round
> Cosmetic wedge sponge
> Craft glue
> Flower-shaped paper cutouts

> Jewelry finding: pin back
> Paper plate
> Pipe cleaner
> Scrap paper
> Spray adhesive
> Ultra-fine glitter: multiple colors

Instructions

Pour small puddle of paint on plate. Dip cosmetic wedge sponge into paint and pounce off excess. Dab paint onto both sides of flower cutouts. Set aside to dry.

Spray one side of flowers with adhesive. Coat with glitter. Shake excess onto scrap paper and pour back into container. If desired, add additional darker color of glitter along edges of petals. Repeat to create four layers. Gently bend up edges of flowers to give more dimension to each layer.

To create beaded stamen, dip end of pipe cleaner into glue. Insert glued end into bead. Glue crystal on end of bead. Set aside to dry.

Insert pipe cleaner stamen through smallest flower first, graduating up to largest flower. Coil pipe cleaner at back to secure in place. Glue on pin back.

100

Initial Charm

Materials

> Craft glue
> Craft paper wire
> Embossing heat gun
> Embossing ink
> Embossing powder: gold and copper
> Jewelry findings: jump ring, necklace chain
> Paper: heavy textured handmade paper, neutral colors
> Pliers
> Scissors
> Small hole punch or embroidery needle
> Tweezers

Above: Craft paper wire and heavy textured paper are used to create this pendant.

Left: Embossing powders along the edges of handmade papers add color and dimension to your Initial Charm Pendant.

Instructions

Form craft paper wire into initial with pliers. Coat with embossing ink. Sprinkle with embossing powder. Hold with tweezers and melt powder with embossing gun. Repeat to coat entire initial.

Cut paper into medallion shape. Emboss edge with copper embossing powder. Cut second paper into medallion shape. Emboss edge with gold embossing powder.

Glue medallions together. Glue initial on top medallion. Punch hole at top of medallion. Insert jump ring. Attach to necklace chain.

Heart Charms

Materials

> Cording: gold
> Craft wire: thin silver
> Embossing heat gun
> Embossing ink: silver
> Heart clips

> Jewelry findings: earring backs, earring clips, toggle necklace closure
> Jewelry glue
> Paper hearts
> Quick-dry glue

> Scissors
> Spacer beads: silver
> Thick embossing powder: silver
> Tweezers

Instructions

Apply embossing ink to paper heart. Sprinkle with embossing powder. Melt powder with embossing gun.

While powder is still hot and melted, press in heart clip, using tweezers for placement. Repeat on back of heart. Create two embossed hearts for each charm.

Cut wire to 1" and fold in half. Twist ends, creating loop. Glue two embossed hearts together with wire loop in between. Set aside to dry.

Top: Heart shapes are available in wire and paper forms. Plain hearts can be embellished with silver embossing ink.

Above: Earrings are created in the same manner as the necklace charms.

Thread on focal charm. Find center of cording and knot to hold charm in place. Continue to add spacer beads and charms, knotting to keep them in place on cord. Attach necklace closure.

Earrings are created in same manner; however, do not glue wire loop in between. Glue on earring backs with jewelry glue.

Left: Add a dab of glue to your knotted ribbon to hold securely to toggle closure.

Left: Heart clips give this necklace a whimsical look while thick embossing powder adds textural interest.

Small die-cut tags and decorative paper clips in the shapes of hearts are an attractive combination of paper and metal. The tags have been embossed with heavy silver powder.

Epoxy Flower

CHOKER & EARRINGS

Materials

> Craft glue

> Epoxy glue

> Jewelry findings: earring backs, necklace closure

> Needle and thread

> Paper flowers: small

> Pliers

> Scrap paper

> Ultra-fine crystal glitter: gold and white

> Vintage ribbon

> Waxed paper

Instructions

Pour generous puddle of epoxy glue onto waxed paper. Hold tip of flower with pliers and dip into epoxy. Hold flower over scrap paper and sprinkle with white glitter. Set on non-stick surface to dry. Sprinkle gold glitter on green leaves of flower. Repeat to create 5 epoxy flowers.

Pour extra glitter back into glitter container. Glue 3 flowers evenly spaced onto ribbon. Set aside to dry. Stitch necklace closure onto ribbon. For earrings, glue on earring backs with craft glue.

Top: Velvet ribbon and paper flowers are married to create this beautiful choker.

Above: The pretty flowers take on a translucent effect when coated with epoxy.

Left: Glue posts onto the backs of a set of flowers to create fanciful earrings.

104

Left: Ribbon takes on a new personality when decorated with sparkling paper flowers.

When creating jewelry with paper, materials make the difference between ordinary and exquisite. Vintage velvet ribbon is a beautiful base for paper flowers coated with epoxy, which strengthens and preserves the blooms.

Scrapbook Tags

Above: Paper tags, found in the scrap-booking section of craft stores, make fun pendants for these easy necklace and earrings sets.

Right: Some paper tags come ready to go or you can add your own alphabet letter words.

Materials

> Beads: glass (ladybug, hearts, round, flat), metal
> Jewelry findings: earring hooks, eye pins, eyelets, jump rings, necklace closures
> Scrapbook tags
> Sheer ribbon

Instructions

Necklace

Attach eyelet to tag. Attach large jump ring to paper tag. Find center of ribbon and thread through jump ring.

Thread both ends of ribbon through bead of choice. At approximately 1" intervals, tie knot in ribbon, thread on decorative bead, and tie knot in ribbon close to bead. Repeat every 1" until end of necklace. Attach necklace closure to end of ribbons.

Earrings

Attach eyelet to tag. Attach jump ring through tag. Thread beads onto eye pin. Cut eye pin to proper length and form end into loop. Attach one end to jump ring and one end to earring hoop.

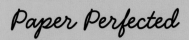

*Left: Attach scrapbook page paper
tags with jump rings to sheer
ribbon and you have an instant
necklace and earrings set. Glass
beads are held in place between
knots in the ribbon.*

Paper tags may be purchased in many shapes.
Another option is to use die cuts or cut shapes out
freehand. Using a unique shape such as elongated
hearts will give your jewelry pieces original flair.

Above: The Flower Drop is created with a vellum tag, a flower sticker, and embossing ink.

Necklace

Materials

> Elastic beading cord

> Hole punch

> Needle: large

> Paper: assorted colored cardstock

> Scissors

> Seed beads

Instructions

Create about 100 paper punches with colored paper and hole punch. Punch hole in center of paper punches with large needle.

Thread punches onto elastic cord in groups of 5-10, using seed beads as spacers. Tie ends of cord into knot; trim ends with scissors. To make bracelet, follow instructions above, using about half the number of paper punches.

Flower Drop

Materials

> Craft glue

> Crystal sparkle embossing powder

> Embossing heat gun

> Embossing ink

> Flower sticker

> Flower vellum tag

> Jewelry finding: jump ring

> Ultra-fine glitter: silver

Instructions

Press sticker onto center of tag. Apply embossing ink to center of flower and sprinkle with embossing powder. Melt powder with embossing gun. Apply dabs of glue to metal rim and sprinkle with glitter. Set aside to dry. Attach to necklace with jump ring.

Paper Perfected

· · · · · · · · · · ·

Punching In

Any youngster who is learning how to use a needle and thread can put their newly developed sewing skills to creative use with this project. That is, of course, after they have had some fun punching holes in colorful paper. Whether it's plain and bright cardstock colors or funky prints, this simple yet playful design is perfect for kids of all ages. Small seed beads provide the spacers on these designs.

Left: Colorful hole punches are fun to make, especially when you string assorted colors for this Paper Punches Necklace and Bracelet set.

A hundred paper punches in a variety of bright colors strung on elastic is a fun and easy project. An embellished flower tag gives this necklace a cheerful focal point.

Paper Words

Materials

> Cardboard shapes

> Craft glue

> Crystal sparkle
  embossing powder

> Embossing heat gun

> Embossing ink

> Fine-tip paintbrush

> Flower stickers

> Jewelry findings:
  tie tack pins

> Paper paint: colors of
  your choice

> Scrapbook alphabet letters

> Soft, flat bristle bush

> Spray gloss varnish

> Ultra-fine glitter

Instructions

Glue five layers of paper alphabet letters together. Set aside to dry. For pins, paint cardboard shape with solid color. Set aside to dry.

Paint patterned design on cardboard shape with fine-tip paintbrush. Set aside to dry. Paint alphabet letters solid color. Set aside to dry.

Top: Alphabet letters and colorful cardstock are used to create these lapel pins.

Above: A fanciful piece of scrapbook paper serves as the perfect background for this pin.

Paint patterned design on letters with fine-tip paintbrush. Glue letters in place on cardboard shape. Apply one coat of spray gloss varnish. Set aside to dry. Repeat for desired finish.

To create initial pin, follow previous instructions for making individual letters. Add flower sticker to top of initial. Apply spray gloss finish. Let dry overnight. Glue tie tack pin to back of letter.

Left: Scrapbook letters and flowers create a pretty initial pin-turned-placecard embellishment just for the girls.

110

Left: Spell out your affections and sentiments with layered scrapbook letters, which can be detailed with easy paint patterns.

Sometimes one word says it all. Die-cut words and letters are available at craft stores or can be custom cut at a local scrapbook store.

Garden of Flowers

Top: Paper flowers and leaves, ribbon, and jewelry findings make up this set.

Above: This necklace is a variation of the Garden of Flowers Necklace.

Necklace

Materials

> Beads: rhinestones, small iridescent, small pearls
> Craft glue
> Jewelry finding: necklace closure
> Narrow soft, flat bristle brush
> Palette or foam plate
> Paper flowers and leaves

> Paper gloss: clear
> Rubber bands: small
> Satin ribbon: 3 complementary colors and textures
> Thread: metallic gold or silver
> Toothpick
> Waxed paper

Instructions

Place paper flower and leaf shapes on waxed paper. Place puddle of paper gloss onto palette. Paint beads with paper gloss on palette.

Dip end of brush into paper gloss and brush onto paper shapes. If desired, glue small rhinestones in center of flowers. Set aside to dry. For glossier effect, repeat with second coat of painted beads. Set aside to dry overnight.

Braid ribbons and trims to desired length. Wrap small rubber bands around ends to hold ribbons in place. *Note:* For broader gluing surface, braid center section of ribbons loose and flat for approximately 3".

Remove paper shapes from waxed paper. Dip end of toothpick into glue and place small amount of glue on back of shape. Place in desired pattern on braided necklace.

Continue to glue paper shapes in layers to build up finished design. If desired, glue small pearls randomly throughout necklace design. Set aside to dry. Attach necklace closure.

Left: Once destined for a scrapbook, this garden of paper flowers blooms on a braided ribbon necklace.

Dimensional paper flower embellishments take on the look of china when covered in paper gloss. Adding crystals and pearls to the center of the flowers adds the feel of fine jewelry. For the best effect, use Swarovski crystals.

113

Earrings

Materials

> Beads: Swarovski crystals

> Craft glue

> Jewelry findings: earring posts

> Paper flowers and leaves

Instructions

Glue paper shapes onto earring posts. Set aside to dry. Tuck in small paper leaves at back of flowers with glue. Glue one Swarovski crystal to center of each paper shape. Set aside to dry completely.

Lapel Pin

Materials

> Beads: metallic, rhinestones, or Swarovski crystals

> Craft glue

> Jewelry finding: filigree metal pin back

> Paintbrush

> Paper gloss

> Paper flowers and leaves

Instructions

Cluster about a dozen paper flowers on a filigree metal pin back. Glue metallic beads or rhinestones to center of flowers. Tuck in small paper leaves at back of pin with glue. Brush on paper gloss; set aside to dry completely.

Top: The paper flower centers also can be embellished with rhinestones or pearls.

Above: Clustered on a filigree metal finding, this floral bouquet makes a pretty lapel pin.

Gallery of Decorative Papers

Every so often we come across dazzling paper designs —some may adorn scrapbook pages, others may have been used in origami projects. Our affection for ephemera—whether it is vintage chic or bold and funky— is growing, and paper suppliers are answering our call for fanciful designs. Since not all papers featured in projects throughout this book are readily available, we've decided to provide a few of our favorites. Our hope is that you mix and match the papers and elements provided—or search out your own at craft and hobby stores—to create beautiful paper jewelry that fits your style and personality. Enjoy!

Birthday Greetings

BIRTHDAY GREETINGS

To wish you a Birthday of gladness
With never a cloud in the skies,
And may every moment of sadness,
Prove only a joy in disguise.

A happy Birthday

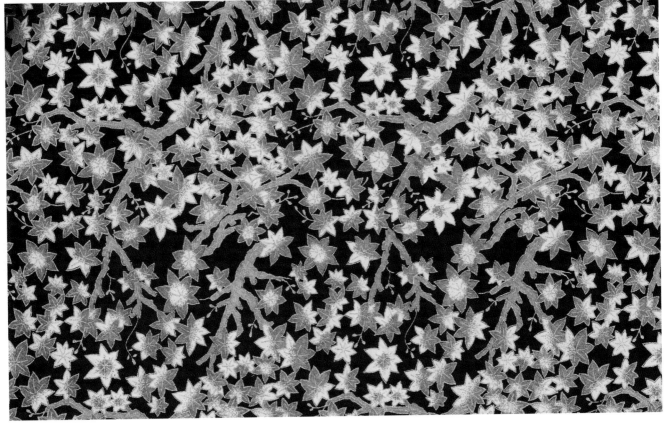

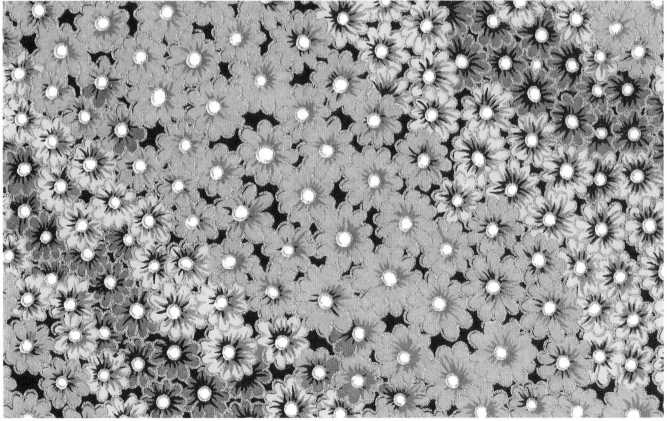

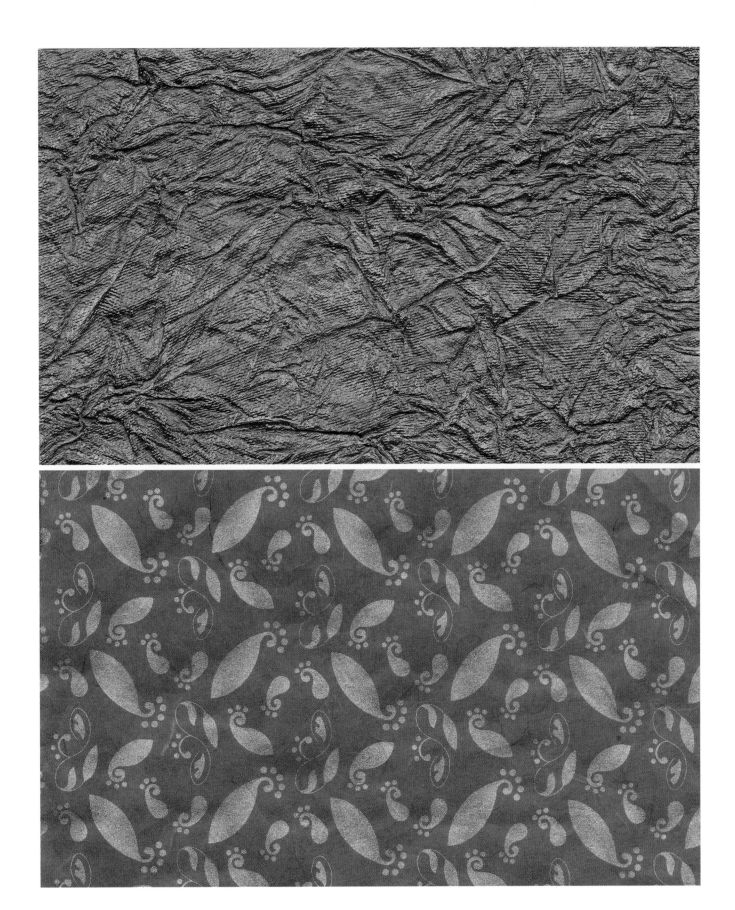

Credits

A RED LIPS 4 COURAGE BOOK

Red Lips 4 Courage Communications, Inc.
Eileen Cannon Paulin, Catherine Risling,
Rebecca Ittner, Jayne Cosh
8502 E. Chapman Ave., 303
Orange, CA 92869
www.redlips4courage.com

BOOK EDITOR

Catherine Risling

BOOK DESIGNER

Deborah Kehoe, Lynn Lantz
Kehoe + Kehoe Design Associates, Inc.
Burlington, VT

PHOTOGRAPHER

Zac Williams

PHOTO STYLIST

Kim Monkres

Acknowledgments

DESIGNERS

Heidi Borchers
www.acreativespark.com

Candace Liccione
www.wyeriverdesigns.com

Tiffany Windsor
www.creativemavens.com
www.inspiredathome.com

PRODUCTS

Acrylic paint
Delta Technical Coatings
www.deltacrafts.com

Beads
A Creative Spark
www.acreativespark.com

Blue Moon Beads
www.bluemoonbeads.com

Michaels Arts & Crafts
www.michaels.com

San Gabriel Bead Company
www.beadcompany.com

Casting paper
Arnold Grummer
www.arnoldgrummer.com

Craft glue
Weldbond
www.franktross.com

Craft wire
Artistic Wire
www.artisticwire.com

Decoupage glue
Delta Technical Coatings
www.deltacrafts.com

Die-cut embellishments
Jolee's Boutique
www.eksuccess.com

E-6000 strong-hold glue
Eclectic Products
www.eclecticproducts.com

Embossing supplies
Suze Weinberg
www.schmoozewithsuze.com

Epoxy glue
Environmental Technology Inc.
www.eti-usa.com

Foil/foiling glue
Delta Technical Coatings
www.deltacrafts.com

Glitter
Art Glitter
www.artglitter.com

Gold leaf paste
Rub 'n' Buff
www.amaco.com

Metallic leaf flakes
Mona Lisa Products
www.houstonart.com

Metallic ribbon tubing
San Gabriel Bead Company
www.beadcompany.com

Mini frame pendant
Tall Mouse Crafts
www.tallmouse.com

Origami and handmade papers
Aitoh
www.aitoh.com

Paper gloss
Delta Paint Jewels
www.deltacrafts.com

Paper paint
Delta Paint for Paper
www.deltacrafts.com

Permanent stamping ink
Delta Pure Color Pigment Ink
www.deltacrafts.com

Quick-dry glue
Aleene's Quick-Dry Glue
www.duncancrafts.com

Rubber stamps
Delta/Rubber Stampede
www.deltacrafts.com

Spray varnish
Delta Indoor/Outdoor Spray Varnish
www.deltacrafts.com

Ultra-thick embossing powder and melting pot
Suze Weinberg
www.schmoozewithsuze.com

Watercolor paper
Blick Art Materials
www.dickblick.com

About the Authors

HEIDI BORCHERS

Heidi Borchers has more than 40 years of creative design experience. Cake decorating, flower making, and, as she calls them, "gluing, gluing, and more gluing" classes as a child at her mother's store really "cemented" her creative expression. At the age of 18, Heidi took over the management of her mother's retail store and soon opened her own retail/wholesale mail-order craft business, which she operated for 20 years. She is the author of more than 100 hardcover and softcover craft books. She is a regular contributing designer to several contemporary craft and lifestyle magazines. Heidi was featured on Aleene's Creative Living television show, where she served as co-host and creative designer for more than 15 years. During that same time, Heidi and her daughter, Starr Hall, teamed up to write and publish *Where Do Angels Buy Their Clothes?* followed by two more popular children's books, *Angel Food—What Do Angels Eat?* and *Jopalbers and Goodles.* This busy artist and grandmother can be found daily at her newest venture, a Creative Spark, located in the quaint village of Cambria, California. At this funky, contemporary design studio, visitors can drop in and mosaic and paint their own pottery and create jewelry, collages, and more.

CANDACE LICCIONE

Creativity has been a life-long journey for this talented and artistic visionary. Working in her mother's family business as a young child, Candace remembers taking every class that was taught in her mother's store. Perhaps it was her experiences in making artificial flowers that blossomed into her love for nature, plants, and herbs. In the 1980s, Candace opened her own retail gift store, where her creative expertise expanded into imaginative window displays and stunning interior store displays. In the mid-1990s, Candace relocated her family to a seven-acre herb farm and opened her herbal and garden sanctuary to the public for educational tours and herbal classes. Students learned how to press and preserve flowers, and make sachets and aromatherapy potpourri, herbal vinegars, soap, paper, aromatherapy, and more. This garden sanctuary provided Candace with the forum to share her gift for helping others recognize their life options. As a life counselor, Candace taught others how to create the atmosphere of sanctuary in their lives and homes. In 2004, Candace opened her newest store, Wye River Design, a contemporary design studio in Grasonville, Maryland, where visitors can stop by and get creative making Candace's creative project of the week, mosaic, or craft jewelry.

TIFFANY WINDSOR

Tiffany Windsor has mastered the art of creative living. Born into an artistic, entrepreneurial family, she found success expressing her talents in many different arenas early in life. Tiffany grew up transforming everyday objects into artistic creations, bejeweling cigar boxes and designing chenille treasures to her heart's content. As an author, storeowner, and television producer, Tiffany has been sharing inspiring ideas for the home and heart for more than a decade. She hosted *Aleene's Creative Living* on The Nashville Network and *Craft, Home, and Style* on The Hallmark Channel, authored numerous books, and launched several online women's magazines. Tiffany wrote and hosted her first prime-time special, *The Magic of Christmas*, that aired on TNN in 1998. The one-hour program featured exquisite holiday decorations, celebrity interviews, cooking, and last-minute crafting ideas for the holidays. In 2003, Tiffany joined Delta Technical Coatings as Director of Consumer Inspiration. Her creative energies were focused on inspiring and educating consumers on the fun of crafting and creative expression. In 2005, Tiffany launched Creative Mavens Retreats, bringing women together through her online magazine, www.homespirations.com, for inspiring and creative retreats.

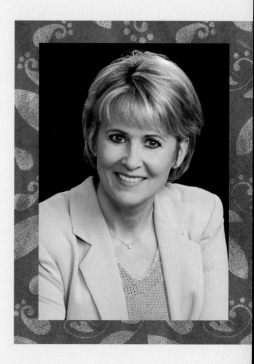

METRIC EQUIVALENCY CHARTS

inches to millimeters and centimeters
mm-millimeters cm-centimeters

inches	mm	cm	inches	cm	inches	cm
⅛	3	0.3	9	22.9	30	76.2
¼	6	0.6	10	25.4	31	78.7
½	13	1.3	12	30.5	33	83.8
⅝	16	1.6	13	33.0	34	86.4
¾	19	1.9	14	35.6	35	88.9
⅞	22	2.2	15	38.1	36	91.4
1	25	2.5	16	40.6	37	94.0
1 ¼	32	3.2	17	43.2	38	96.5
1 ½	38	3.8	18	45.7	39	99.1
1 ¾	44	4.4	19	48.3	40	101.6
2	51	5.1	20	50.8	41	104.1
2 ½	64	6.4	21	53.3	42	106.7
3	76	7.6	22	55.9	43	109.2
3 ½	89	8.9	23	58.4	44	111.8
4	102	10.2	24	61.0	45	114.3
4 ½	114	11.4	25	63.5	46	116.8
5	127	12.7	26	66.0	47	119.4
6	152	15.2	27	68.6	48	121.9
7	178	17.8	28	71.1	49	124.5
8	203	20.3	29	73.7	50	127.0

yards to meters

yards	meters	yards	meters	yards	meters	yards	meters	yards	meters
⅛	0.11	2 ⅛	1.94	4 ⅛	3.77	6 ⅛	5.60	8 ⅛	7.43
¼	0.23	2 ¼	2.06	4 ¼	3.89	6 ¼	5.72	8 ¼	7.54
⅜	0.34	2 ⅜	2.17	4 ⅜	4.00	6 ⅜	5.83	8 ⅜	7.66
½	0.46	2 ½	2.29	4 ½	4.11	6 ½	5.94	8 ½	7.77
⅝	0.57	2 ⅝	2.40	4 ⅝	4.23	6 ⅝	6.06	8 ⅝	7.89
¾	0.69	2 ¾	2.51	4 ¾	4.34	6 ¾	6.17	8 ¾	8.00
⅞	0.80	2 ⅞	2.63	4 ⅞	4.46	6 ⅞	6.29	8 ⅞	8.12
1	0.91	3	2.74	5	4.57	7	6.40	9	8.23
1 ⅛	1.03	3 ⅛	2.86	5 ⅛	4.69	7 ⅛	6.52	9 ⅛	8.34
1 ¼	1.14	3 ¼	2.97	5 ¼	4.80	7 ¼	6.63	9 1/4	8.46
1 ⅜	1.26	3 ⅜	3.09	5 ⅜	4.91	7 ⅜	6.74	9 ⅜	8.57
1 ½	1.37	3 ½	3.20	5 ½	5.03	7 ½	6.86	9 ½	8.69
1 ⅝	1.49	3 ⅝	3.31	5 ⅝	5.14	7 ⅝	6.97	9 ⅝	8.80
1 ¾	1.60	3 ¾	3.43	5 ¾	5.26	7 ¾	7.09	9 ¾	8.92
1 ⅞	1.71	3 ⅞	3.54	5 ⅞	5.37	7 ⅞	7.20	9 ⅞	9.03
2	1.83	4	3.66	6	5.49	8	7.32	10	9.14

Index